T0247761

# DECISIVE
# BATTLES
# IN
# CHINESE
# HISTORY

The Four Generals of Zhongxing with their four attendants, painted by Southern Song dynasty artist Liu Songnian in 1214. In order to show the most detail, the painting has been divided in the middle. The generals at top are from the left, Yue Fei (second) and Zhang Jun (fourth); at the bottom, Han Shizhong (first) and Liu Guangshi (third).

# DECISIVE BATTLES

# IN

# CHINESE HISTORY

## MORGAN DEANE

WESTHOLME
Yardley

Westholme Publishing, LLC
904 Edgewood Road
Yardley, Pennsylvania 19067
Visit our Web site at www.westholmepublishing.com

ISBN: 978-1-59416-289-3
Also available as an eBook.

Printed in the United States of America.

# CONTENTS

# LIST OF MAPS

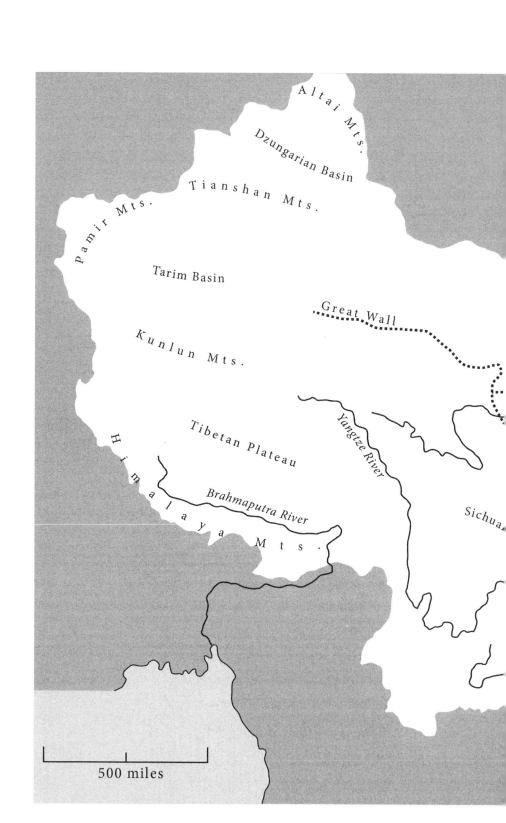

Altai Mts.

Dzungarian Basin

Tianshan Mts.

Pamir Mts.

Tarim Basin

Great Wall

Kunlun Mts.

Tibetan Plateau

Yangtze River

Brahmaputra River

H i m a l a y a  M t s .

Sichua

500 miles

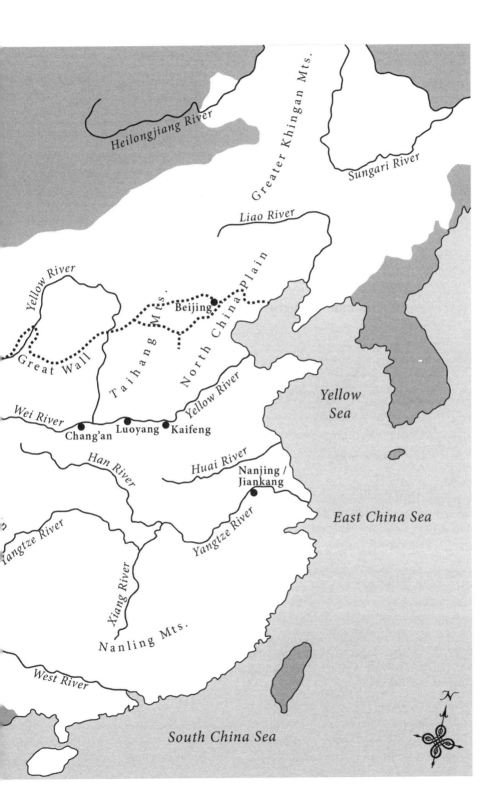

# Imperial Dynasties of China*

| NAME | PERIOD |
| --- | --- |
| Qin | 221 BC–207 BC |
| Western Han | c. 206 BC–8 |
| Xin | 9–23 |
| Eastern Han | 25–220 |
| Three Kingdoms | 220–280 |
| Western Jin | 265–317 |
| Eastern Jin | 317–420 |
| Southern and Northern | 420–589 |
| Sui | 581–618 |
| Tang | 618–907 |
| Five Dynasties and Ten Kingdoms | 907–960 |
| Kingdom of Dali | 937–1253 |
| Northern Song | 960–1127 |
| Southern Song | 1127–1279 |
| Liao | c. 907–1125 |
| Jin | 1115–1234 |
| Western Xia | 1038–1227 |
| Western Liao | 1124–1218 |
| Yuan | 1271–1368 |
| Ming | 1368–c. 1662 |
| Qing | c. 1636–1911 |

*Preceding the imperial dynasties were the ancient dynasties of Xia, Shang, Eastern and Western Zhou, and the Spring and Autumn and Warring States periods.

# INTRODUCTION

[The] period of sixty years . . . which has just ended, was probably the most momentous for China, if not for the world at large; for it was in 1839 [the First Opium War] that the difficulties of intercourse between the East and the West came to the first crisis. The year 1899 seems to mark another crisis, which, as regards the integrity of the Chinese problem, may prove final. Yet the situation in Far Eastern Asia was grasped by only a few Western observers before 1895, when the struggle for suzerainty over Korea revealed the helplessness of China, and lifted Japan to a seat in the council of Powers. Though worsted in two foreign wars and nearly wrecked by an internal convulsion, the government of the "Son of Heaven" had learned nothing new and forgotten nothing old. . . . Each government has been bullying Beijing in its turn, demanding this or that contract or concession with or without the color of a pretext. . . . Is it for the benefit of the United States to deal with China as a vast unit under her native flag, or as fragments under many flags? That is what we have to decide.

—"The Break-Up of China, and Our Interest in It"
*Atlantic Monthly*, August 1899

THIS AMERICAN WRITER at the transition to the twentieth century illustrated the compromised condition of China at the time and a significant reason why China became susceptible to being stereotyped. The concern of the author of this article is how Americans should receive their share of the commercial interest in China. It is a given that China is weak, helpless, and "had learned nothing new and forgotten nothing old." The relative powerlessness of China during a period of Western strength is one of the many reasons that the study of Chinese military history has been neglected. But there are additional problems and barriers.

Western historians who master difficult Eastern languages still face a challenging time. There are relatively few primary and archived sources outside of Beijing or Nanjing. For translations and non-Chinese language histories, spelling differs from book to book depending on the system of transliteration used. (Except for relatively well-known people and places such as Nationalist leader Chiang Kai-shek, I use the Pinyin system. It abandons diacritics and is what most modern scholars use.) If a researcher is able to access Chinese language material, trying to find unbiased primary sources with detailed descriptions of battles is rather difficult until one reaches the modern age. The result is that the lack of introductory or more advanced material for students and scholars reinforces the perception that Chinese military history is unimportant. The seemingly "unimportant" field doesn't inspire more to research it, and combined with the difficulty of mastering the language and accessing archived sources, it means the field remains under examined.

The study of Chinese military history also faces steep hurdles from Chinese cultural values and the way events were transmitted to the West. The first Westerners who had significant academic engagement in China were Jesuit missionaries, beginning in the sixteenth century. They interacted with Chinese elites who also disdained war and emphasized cultural values over military ones. The Jesuits sent back to the West the stories of Chinese civil virtue and martial impotence. (Ironically, Jesuit cannon-making skills were among the most sought after technologies the Chinese wished to obtain.) Chinese scholars emphasized the strongly held cultural values that helped create the great dynasties and almost completely ignored the equally important role of warfare. From the first dynasty of China in 221 BC, civilian leaders exercised political dominance over the military. Though outranked by their civilian counterparts, the military men held great power, and it was the use or lack of military power that

brought about the rise and fall of dynasties. Many Chinese leaders adopted passive or nonviolent ways to subdue their enemies,
such as marriage proposals or generous trade agreements. But
these were often done as a way to compensate for military weakness. During times of martial strength, Chinese leaders preferred
pacification campaigns because they had the means to carry
them out; during times of weakness, in contrast, they often
adopted other methods. But it was the relative martial strength
of the dynasty, its ability to project power, and other practical
considerations that often determined strategy, not an overwhelming cultural preference for pacifism.[1]

There are many books about major or decisive battles, but few
have more than a handful of non-Western battles, nor do they
examine the battles with the expertise of a Chinese military historian. If they do include non-Western battles, it is usually because of their association with (and defeat by) the West. In *A
History of War in 100 Battles*, for example, only four battles
do not have a European or American opponent, and only six
are from the Southern Hemisphere.[2] Another book presented itself as the authoritative guide to battles in world history but did-
n't include a single section devoted to Chinese history, the index
did not include an entry on China, and the book contains only
scant references to Japanese history.[3]
   It is true that China entered a long period of military weakness at the same time the West was expanding its influence glob-
ally, and there is significant question about its capabilities even
today. But the picture is far more complicated than the West
dominating and China trying to keep up. China has one of the
oldest civilizations and has a claim to some of the longest continuous cultural traditions. It fielded armies as big as half a million soldiers during the Warring States period, or roughly the
same time that Rome was little more than a collection of huts
on a few hillsides. China invented key technologies such as the
crossbow and gunpowder. During a time when America was a

small nation clinging to the Eastern Seaboard, China extended its rule over hundreds of thousands of square miles with hundreds of millions of people. It also has a history that seems almost cyclical at points, where a strong dynasty would eventually collapse, followed by a period of weakness and then consolidation and expansion under a new emperor. It had the singularly unfortunate timing to enter a period of weakness and fail to industrialize during a period of rapid change in the West. For example, at the start of the Opium War in 1839 (see chapter 10), the Chinese armies possessed fairly modern weapons and defensive fortifications but could not keep pace. The British fielded their first ironclad the very year that war started and had several other advantages that unfairly cast the Chinese as backward and hopelessly inferior.

This book is designed for general readers and students to learn major themes and issues in Chinese history and military history through key moments of conflict. Each chapter starts with an account of a battle and its immediate political and military impact. It then broadens its focus to present an overview of events that led to and were impacted by the battle. I have chosen battles that I believe best highlight Chinese strategy, military culture, tactics, weapons, and geography. In additon, I have attempted to consolidate information contained in widely disparate sources, from obscure academic journals to rare monographs to other secondary sources, as well as select primary sources. I hope readers will find this an approachable introduction to major themes in Chinese military history and, by extension, Chinese history.

# THE BATTLE OF MALING

## 342 BC

Clearly observe the enemy's coming and going, advancing and withdrawing. Investigate his movements and periods at rest, whether they speak about portents, what the officers and troops report. If the Three Armies are exhilarated [and] the officers and troops fear the laws; respect the general's commands; rejoice with each other in destroying the enemy; boast to each other about their courage and ferocity; and praise each other for their awesomeness and martial demeanor— these are indications of a strong enemy.

If the Three Armies have been startled a number of times, the officers and troops no longer maintaining good order; they terrify each other [with stories about] the enemy's strength; they speak to each other about the disadvantages; they anxiously look about at each other, listening carefully; they talk incessantly of ill omens, myriad mouths confusing each other; they fear neither laws nor orders and do not regard their general seriously—these are indications of weakness.

*—The Six Secret Teachings of Tai Kong*

P ANG JUAN WAS INCENSED. In 342 BC, he was a few days away from taking the capital of his enemy, the Han. But the state of Qi had finally invaded on behalf of its Han ally. The former had delayed out of political considerations. It wanted the two other states—the state of Wei, with armies led by Pang Juan, and its ally the Han—to deplete their reserves fighting against each other. But now the Qi saw the capital of their ostensible ally about to fall and made their move to clean up the rival army and be the strongest partner in their alliance. Sun Bin, the commander of the Qi, knew that Pang Juan was angry and aggressive. He likely read the passage in general and military strategist Sunzi's (Sun-Tzu) book about the commander's anger being "hot" and exploited it to his advantage. Instead of directly attacking the newly invading Wei forces, Sun Bin aimed for their capital and lured them out.

But these generals had faced each other before. Pang Juan knew that Sun Bin had likely set an ambush, so he ordered his troops to go around the Qi force and avoid the ambush. The Wei troops moved quickly, taking circuitous routes as they hunted down the Qi forces of Sun Bin. But Sun Bin had more tricks up his sleeve. He avoided attacking the swiftly moving forces right away. Instead he let the Wei troops get close, and then backtracked to his own lands. When camped for the night, he ordered his troops to light fewer and fewer cooking stoves. The first day he had one hundred thousand stoves lit. The second day he ordered fifty thousand lit. And the final day he allowed only twenty thousand lit. This suggested to observers, again following the instructions of classical military texts to observe the enemy's camp for signs, that Qi troops were deserting in droves. At this sign, Pang Juan sent a small and elite cavalry force to hunt down the apparently fleeing soldiers. This unit had incredibly high morale, as it was responsible for large victories to date for the Wei forces.

To better sell the story that his troops were panicking, Sun Bin ordered his soldiers to abandon some of their artillery pieces as well, as though they had fled so quickly in a state of panic that they couldn't take the pieces with them. Finally, Sun found a small and heavily wooded pass to his liking. As the story goes, he calculated that Pang Juan would reach the pass by nightfall.

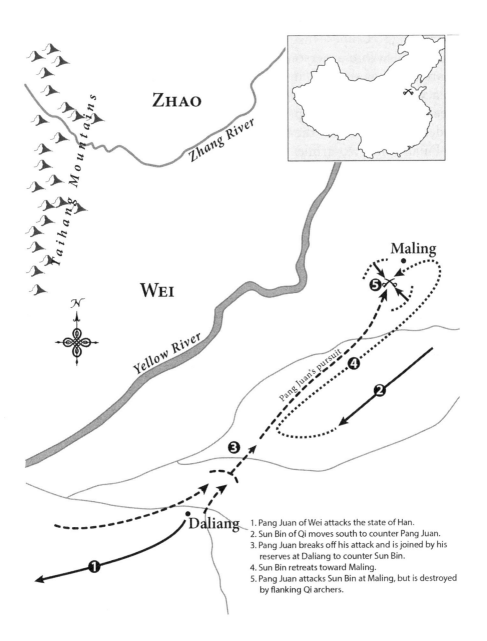

The Battle of Maling, 342 BC.

1. Pang Juan of Wei attacks the state of Han.
2. Sun Bin of Qi moves south to counter Pang Juan.
3. Pang Juan breaks off his attack and is joined by his reserves at Daliang to counter Sun Bin.
4. Sun Bin retreats toward Maling.
5. Pang Juan attacks Sun Bin at Maling, but is destroyed by flanking Qi archers.

According to Chinese historians, he cut down a tree, shaved the bark, and wrote a personal message for Pang based on their shared days as students in the same class.[1] It should have acted as a warning—"Pang Juan shall die in Malingdao, under this tree"—yet it acted as a prophecy. Pang Juan saw the message, ordered it scraped off the tree, and continued his pursuit.

Finally the two armies clashed near Maling. Sun Bin positioned ten thousand archers in the trees beside the road, and they opened fire on the cavalry moving along the narrow pass. The first wave of Wei soldiers quickly fell in the surprise onslaught. Those following the slaughtered vanguard quickly charged in despite their surprise at the strength and size of Qi forces. Pang Juan and his soldiers fought with spirit, but they quickly fell to the Qi. The sources variously say that Pang Juan committed suicide when he saw defeat at hand, or he was shot and killed early in the battle.

Qi forces quickly overran much of the Wei and captured their prince. Wei power declined precipitously after the defeat at Maling. Qi became one of the largest and most powerful states of the Warring States period until it was defeated by the Qin (pronounced Chin), who founded the Qin dynasty in 221 BC and lent their name to the region we now call China.

This battle highlights various important factors related to Chinese history. Above all, it shows the already advanced state of Chinese military thought. These two forces performed rather sophisticated maneuvers and countermaneuvers in order to outsmart their opponents before the battle had even started. The writings of various political, religious, and military thinkers were widely disseminated and rather influential in this period (and for all of Chinese history up to the present). They fought with cavalry, showing a departure from early periods in Chinese history. They had rather large armies that were conscripted, trained, armed, and supplied by sophisticated bureaucracies. They had capable leaders who represented a skilled class of literate military specialists. And the results of these battles quickly led to the formation of the Chinese imperial state.

THE FIRST KINGDOMS

The arable land around the Yellow River where the states of Wei and Qi fought constituted an important center of agriculture for early China. There is much more to history than simply feeding people, and though growing grain seems rather pedestrian compared to the great wonders of the ancient world, feeding people is the important first step. The increase in agricultural output around 4000 BC led to surplus food. The extra food created conditions that allowed people to focus on other pursuits than farming. In short, the surplus was the start of a specialist economy, as a state could now support political leaders, full-time armies, artists, scribes, priests, merchants, and lawyers.

By around 2000 BC, this process had created the Xia, Shang, and Zhou dynasties. These dynasties reach back to the earliest recorded histories and even merged with myth and prehistory similar to the ancient Sumerians and Akkadians of Mesopotamia. Only the latter two Chinese dynasties have any solid evidence for their existence.

The three major trends of Shang civilization were writing, bronze working, and the rise of social classes. Shang specialists wrote on bamboo, but none of these writings is known to have survived to the modern day. (This is the same medium that Warring States military theorists wrote on and is often the reason why their sayings are so terse.) The earliest examples of writing were the oracle bones. These were short questions written on bones and then submitted to a deity by priests. The shaman priests then wrote the answers in response. Often these questions focused on matters of war, but they also included hunting predictions and interpretations of heavenly signs. Other questions answered by the oracle bones involved the blessings of heaven on their kingship.

The palace at the ancient capital of Anyang attests to the power of the elites. Since construction of this palace was as labor intensive as the pyramids of ancient Egypt or the ziggurats of Babylon, only a ruling class that had the ability to amass huge amounts of labor could build them. This suggests an advanced society with a distinct ruling class that held most of the political and military power. This palace also contained servants' quarters. Archeologists have uncovered pottery shards that help shed light on the artisan economy. Much like the ability to raise armies and command labor, the surplus in farming allowed the elite class to hire and house artisans.

By 1050 BC, the Shang dynasty succumbed to the western Zhou. The rulers justified their revolution by proclaiming what would become a stereotype used repeatedly by Chinese historians to explain dynastic changes. The stereotype consisted of the following sequence of events: The previous dynasty suffered from a bad last emperor who forfeited his claim to rule through his licentious, excessive lifestyle, defeat in war, and the onerous tax burden he placed upon the people. Then the revolutionary forces cited inauspicious omens that signaled the loss of divine favor. These omens included floods, shooting stars, droughts, and military defeats. By this point, the revolutionaries usually held somewhat independent territories, and the governors, or warlords, of these territories offered relief from taxes and more responsive leadership than the current dynasty, which in turn swelled the governors' forces. The forces of the rival warlords then defeated the ruling dynasty or other contenders for the throne and upon victory proclaimed that they had earned the Mandate of Heaven. This mandate is a Chinese belief that heaven blesses and makes prosper the rulers who are fit to govern. These blessings then flow down to the people to benefit the entire realm.

That is the narrative surrounding the mandate, but it differs slightly from the actual history. In this case, the Shang dynasty overextended itself in campaigns against its nomadic neighbors to the north. Inscriptions from oracle bones suggest the Shang had both positive and negative relations with their neighbors. After the Shangs' ineffective campaigns, the Zhou allied with disaffected city-states and swept aside the former dynasty. They continued many of the Shang patterns of life and rule, yet they still consisted of a small minority among their more-civilized

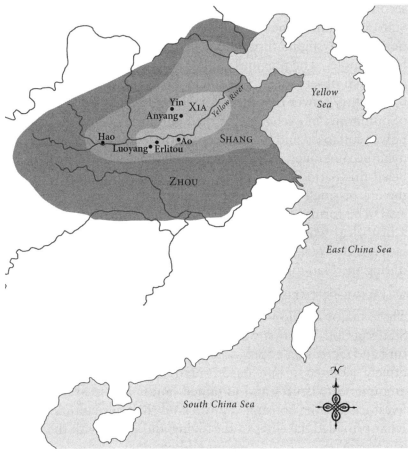

Early Chinese dynasties, c. 2000 BC. Anyang was the earlier capital of the Xia, with Luoyang and other cities gaining prominence as Chinese civilization expanded.

subjects. The Zhou needed a reason for their violent conquest and a foundation for their right to rule. This became the Mandate of Heaven.

By 771 BC, this dynasty also entered a period of decay. The decay of central power led to one of many instances in Chinese history when centrifugal forces created many small independent kingdoms. Barbarians attacked and sacked the primary capital of the western Zhou. Remnants of the political elite fled to the secondary capital at Luoyang, near what became the Warring State Kingdom of the Qi and Wei. (Luoyang would be the location of many fights throughout Chinese history; see chapter 3 for example.) The previous capital remained a center of culture and ritual observances. The rulers, however, were so desperate for military power that the local elites often gained a great deal of autonomy in exchange for their support. Eventually, central power collapsed and local rulers appointed by a central government became rulers of their own small kingdoms. Historians labeled this period of decay the Spring and Autumn period and the era of small independent kingdoms the Warring States period. The former comes from *The Spring and Autumn Annals*, a historical work attributed to Confucius (551–479 BC). The latter is derived from *Records of the Warring States*, written during the Han dynasty.

### WARFARE IN THE WARRING STATES PERIOD

Three major developments marked the entry into the Warring States period. The first was the increasing expansion of agriculture and increasing population. Previously, the cities formed relatively isolated urban oases surrounded by relatively large amounts of pastures and untamed lands. Horse breeding and livestock grazing consumed more land than agriculture. This is what provided the elites of the Shang and Zhou with the means to raise massive chariot armies and conduct aristocratic hunts. During this period, though, farms increasingly replaced pastures, which in turn raised the population. This led to a rise in the number of cities. The increasing population combined with a weak central government led to conflicts over boundaries and prime agricultural land. It also decreased the amount of land that aristocrats could use to support their chariot armies and conduct hunts.

The second major development featured a rise in commerce. Farmers needed roads to transport their products to the markets in timely fashion. Even today this concept allows a customer in Minnesota to buy fresh fruit in December from a local grocer. This also facilitated the transportation of merchants. Tombs of

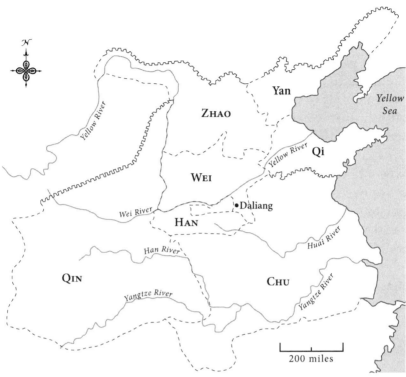

The Warring States, c. 260 BC. The current version of the Great Wall was built in the late sixteenth century, though various walls, trenches, and fortifications were built in the same location going as far back as the Warring States period. The various defensive walls marked the divide between the sedentary northern Chinese and the nomadic steppe groups.

the elites in this period featured bronze bells and mirrors, clay figurines, lacquer boxes, lace, and musical instruments, suggesting a vigorous and surprisingly expansive trade. The merchants then rivaled the nobility in terms of prestige, power, and wealth, which also led to a weakening of central authority. Chinese society consistently marginalized merchants throughout its history, but merchants still played an important role in generating wealth and acting as centers of power. For example, the taxes on these powerful merchants financed the battles fought between warring states, and control of vital trade routes was often the prime strategy in those conflicts.

With the growth in population and increasingly wealthy people, the third major development consisted of the small breakaway states fielding large armies. At a time (500 BC) when Greeks were fighting with armies that measured several thousand, the major Chinese warring states each fielded armies in the hundreds of thousands. For centuries, the elite class fought with bronze weapons in chariots supported by infantry conscripts. By the Warring States period, the armies consisted of mass conscripted infantry with iron weapons, with large crossbow and cavalry components. The chariot lacked the ability to move over rough terrain, needed more land to supply multiple horses for each chariot, and was supplanted by the more nimble cavalry. The ability to use a crossbow without a great deal of training made the weapon ideal for larger conscripted armies. The armies of this size could only be mustered using weapons that required little advanced training. This isn't to say that the armies were poorly trained but that some weapons facilitated larger armies. The crossbow's deadly shot and short range made it ideal for breaking up large masses of opposing infantry.

The democratization of war had several major effects. The old nobility gave way to a rise of professional soldiers and ministers. In place of a feudal duke, the Chinese warring states employed ministers of war. These ministers acted as free agents in much the same way as modern-day athletes. They took their services and particular skill set and worked for the highest bidder. Their knowledge of statecraft, administration, and tax policy helped transform the agricultural states into military powers. The ministers directed the collection of taxes, kept detailed records, levied soldiers (hundreds of thousands of them), advised the king in strategic matters, and selected competent generals.

One of the most famous of these ministers was Master Sun, or Sunzi. His military tract, *The Art of War*, is one of the most famous writings in the world. It contains his advice as a minister of war. The terse text and simple profundity of his statements have led to its wide use and enjoyment not simply in Chinese history but worldwide and continuing to this day. The book emphasized the material and human costs of war. Because of this high cost, the ruler must seek the most expeditious way to either avoid war or achieve victory. This included subterfuge (such as Sun Bin manipulating the number of camping stoves lit), the use of spies, beguiling opponents with women, supplying the enemy with misleading information, and psychologically undoing an opponent through ruses. Ideally, this meant winning a battle without even fighting one; or, if war is imminent, gaining an advantage before the fight. Preparation is essential. The ruler should do everything in order to achieve harmony between the well-being of the people and supplying the army. The ruler should create strategic conditions where defeat is impossible and victory is as sudden, decisive, and easy as water flowing down from the mountain. The book had a Daoist tone as well (see chapter 2), where he described the "formlessness" of an army and the ability to adapt to a wide variety of situations and act in harmony with the situation presented.

This text joined many others such as *The Wuzi* (with a historical author who likely worked for the state of Wei), *The Six Secret Teachings of Tai Kong*, and *The Methods of Suma* that made up the Seven Military Classics of ancient China.[2] Formed in the Song dynasty (960–1279 AD), they acted as primary military education texts for potential leaders. In addition, they contained a great deal of nonmartial thought that reflected the intellectual trends of the Warring States period and much of subsequent Chinese history.

Moreover, the texts represent a moral world view that dominated Chinese battle. Battle included a great deal of practical matters, such as the logistical needs of soldiers and manner of their training. But the texts were also concerned with cosmological matters and references to divination and prognostication. In Chinese thought, battle represented heaven's verdict on a ruler. In the run up to the Battle of Maling, Sun Bin left a moral message for Pang Juan to find, and ignoring it led to the latter's death.

CONCLUSION

The Battle of Maling represents the culmination of a long development in Chinese history. Like other ancient civilizations, Chinese civilization formed around an arable river valley producing a staple crop. The people and rulers created powerful religious and government institutions. By the time of the Warring States period, Chinese warfare was led by a class of literate military specialists producing and circulating profound texts. The armies represented a capable bureaucratic class and government that could raise, equip, train, maintain, and lead large and well-armored forces into combat. The trained military specialists could then command armies in rather complex maneuvers during campaigns that lasted months and ranged over hundreds of miles. They became the basis of a new and stronger government, as well as agents of chaos when that government faltered.

# 2

# THE BATTLE OF RED CLIFFS

## 208

Now take a young fellow who is a bad character. His parents may get angry at him, but he never makes any change. The villagers may reprove him, but he is not moved. His teachers and elders may admonish him, but he never reforms. The loves of his parents, the efforts of the villagers, and the wisdom of his teachers and elders—all the three excellent disciplines are applied to him, and yet not even a hair on his shins is altered. It is only after the district magistrate sends out his soldiers and in the name of the law searches for wicked individuals that the young man becomes afraid and changes his ways and alters his deeds. So while the love of parents is not sufficient to discipline the children, the severe penalties of the district magistrate are. This is because men became naturally spoiled by love, but are submissive to authority. . . .

That being so, rewards should be rich and certain so that the people will be attracted by them; punishments should be severe and definite so that the people will fear them; and laws should be uniform and steadfast so that the people will be familiar with them. Consequently, the sovereign should show no wavering in bestowing rewards and grant no pardon in administering punishments, and he should add honor to reward and disgrace to punishments—when this is done, then both the worthy and the unworthy will want to exert themselves.

—Han Feizi

I lift my drink and sing a song, for who knows if life is short
or long?
Man's life is but the morning dew, past days many, future ones
few.
The melancholy my heart begets, comes from cares I cannot
forget;
What can unravel these woes of mine? I know but one drink—
[The God of] Wine.
Disciples dress in blue, my heart worries for you.
You are the cause, of this song without pause.
Across the bank a deer bleats, in the wild where it eats.
Honored my guests I salute, strike the harp! Play the flute!
Bright is the moon's spark, when can I pick it apart?
Thoughts of you from deep inside, cannot settle, cannot sub-
side.
Friends drop by via a country road, the respect they pay really
shows.
A long due reunion we fest, sharing past stories we possessed.
Stars around the moons are few, southward the crows flew.
Flying with no rest, where shall they nest?
No mountain too steep, no ocean too deep.
Sage pauses [from meals] when guests call, so at his feet the
empire does fall!

—Cao Cao, "Short Song Style"

Cao Cao (155–220) was on an incredible march. Figu-
ratively, he rose from a middle-class leader of a private
band of soldiers to the chancellor and nominal leader of northern China. He led an impressive force of loyal companion soldiers and a polyglot collection of war bands to defeat his
enemies. The Yellow River was the traditional cultural and political center of China, and now he controlled it.

By 208, he was literally marching south to reunite the increasingly shattered remnants of the Han dynasty. The last effective
leader had been deposed by its own leading general, Dong
Zhuo, in 189. The chaotic fighting between rival generals, new
warlords, and those with private armies such as Cao Cao consumed the empire for decades.

Marching south in 208 with a unified north behind him, Cao easily defeated Lui Biao and seized the key Jing Province. This extended his territory from the Han River, a tributary of the Yellow, all the way to the key southern river, the Yangtze. Capturing the vital river base at Jiangling and clearing out the enemy armies around it would grant him control of most of the central Yangtze basin and provide him a dominant position from where he would eliminate the last few rivals to central authority.

Sensing the imminence of Cao's victory, the two southern rivals, Liu Bei and Sun Quan combined their forces to oppose him. They tried to flank Cao's force from the south and east, and ended up meeting at Red Cliffs, along the Yangtze River, in 208. Cao Cao's elite cavalry had pursued the retreating forces of the former governor of Jing Province as far as he could. Cao's forces are said to have numbered eight hundred thousand but likely were no more than two hundred thirty thousand. Of these, about eighty thousand were forcibly conscripted after Cao's recent victory in Jing Province, and the rest were northerners unaccustomed to riverine combat in southern marshes. Most of them had as little as three days of training in naval operations and marine tactics. The opposing force from the south consisted of only fifty thousand soldiers, but they were trained marines with long experience fighting in the environment and ready for amphibious combat. Cao had shown great military acumen in securing the north, but his southern strategy was far simpler. He advanced against the enemy forces arrayed against him and expected his superior numbers would crush his opponents in battle.

With Cao's forces on the north shore of the Yangtze, the combined Liu/Sun force sailed a short distance upstream toward the Red Cliffs. Cao Cao's vanguard was exhausted from its recent chase and reportedly fighting disease picked up from the various marshy bogs through which it had just crossed. A brief opening skirmish ensued, and Cao's force retreated a bit from the north bank of the river. One of the admirals in the southern force feigned surrender to Cao's navy. It looked as though Cao's overwhelming force and previous victories in the province was having a positive effect.

1. The warlord Cao Cao leads his
   to attack the region below th

2. Liu Bei, leader of the eastern
   Cao Cao's attack and is forced

3. Liu Bei's general, Guan Yu, sail
   Liu Bei's son, Liu Qi, brings ad

4. Cao Cao's forces continue to J
   the Yangtze River to attack Wu

5. Han general Zhou Yu leads hi
   join forces with Liu Bei.

6. The Sun and Han allies clash v

7. Defeated, Cao Cao retreats th

8. The Sun and Han allies sail up
   the warlord to flee north, leav
   free from further attacks.

The Battle of Red Cliffs, 208.

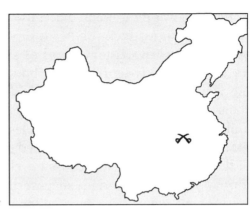

numerically superior forces
Yangtze.
an, falls back in the face of
o retreat after the Battle of Changban.
his forces down the Han River, while
itional reinforcements.
ingling, where they then embark on
in.
Sun troops up the Yangtze where they

ith Cao Cao's army at Red Cliffs.
ough marshland.
he Yangtze to pursue Cao Cao, forcing
ng the area south of the Yangtze River

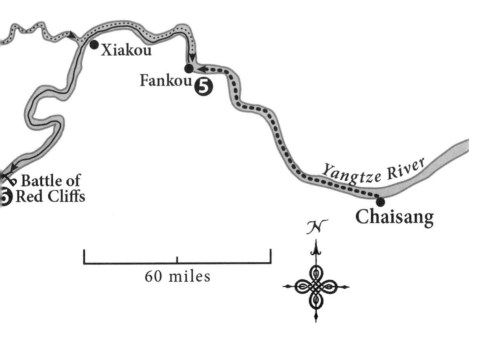

But Cao was disappointed because his opponent was actually launching a fire attack similar to those called for by Sunzi and other classical theorists. Instead of surrendering capital ships, the sailors quickly set fire to dry bundles of reeds and grass on the vessels and then escaped in small boats. The floating fire ships crashed into the fleet Cao needed to cross the river and set it ablaze. The smoke carried for miles, and dozens of ships and thousands of men and horses burned to death. The effectiveness of the attacks was great because Cao had left his ships in a close formation. Some historians suggest this was designed to aid his seasick men and prevent the need for extensive maneuvers.[1] That formation aided the fire attacks a great deal.

Sensing that both the literal and figurative tide had turned against him, Cao ordered a general retreat. But he had to do so along a single road through the same marshes that sickened and exhausted his army in the first place. Heavy rains added to their misery and made the retreat even more precarious. Cao's infantry forces had to carry bundles of reeds to provide enough foundation for the horses to walk on. The enemies pursued Cao so aggressively that many of Cao's cavalry trampled their own soldiers in the retreat.

Cao managed to stabilize his army and the situation in the north, but he lost his momentum and died a few years later. The divided kingdoms continued, and except for a brief respite at the beginning of the third century, China witnessed hundreds of years of chaos. The Battle of Red Cliffs was the most pivotal battle in what the Chinese regard as the romantic Three Kingdoms period (though it is considered part of the early unofficial portion of it). It is one of the most celebrated and reenacted battles in Chinese history, and it marked the permanent end of the Han dynasty, though imperial Confucianism and its cultural influence continued to shape Chinese attitudes and history.[2]

THE ROMANCE OF THE THREE KINGDOMS

The Three Kingdoms period which followed the Han dynasty is considered one of the most bloody in Chinese history. Even though the population declined due to protracted conflict, this is considered one of the most romantic periods in Chinese history. The kingdoms of Wei (ruled by Cao Cao's descendants), Shu, and Wu each ruled a portion of China, and they waged war against each other before finally being consolidated under the Jin dynasty (see chapter 3).

*The Romance of the Three Kingdoms* is attributed to Luo Guanzhong and was written sometime during the fourteenth century. It's a fictionalized account of Chinese history from 169 to 280 AD. Much like *Game of Thrones*, which borrows heavily from the English War of the Roses, the book dramatizes, embellishes, romanticizes, and adds some legendary elements and composite characters to the period.

It starts with the end of the dynasty, when cunning eunuchs and court officials deceive the emperor and punish the good ministers. Finally, the empire collapses from its corruption. The story then follows numerous secondary characters and complex events, but they show many of the common cultural elements in Chinese history. There are evil rebel generals, the forfeiture of rule by unrighteous ministers, Cao Cao escaping two assassination attempts, competing warlords secretly finding and keeping the imperial seal, overambition leading to collapse, and, above all, a great deal of war and battle and conflict between the lofty ideals of Confucianism and the harsh realities of Legalism. Eventually, Sima Yi seizes power from the Cao family and establishes the Jin dynasty.

The book has contributed a number of Chinese proverbs. One—"Every person on the street knows what is in Sima Zhao's mind"—comes from a line uttered by Cao Mao, a descendent of Cao Cao's, who lamented that the ambitions of his adviser (Sima Zhao) were so obvious that everybody knew his mind. It is used in Chinese to describe a person whose ambitions are rather obvious. Another saying is, "Speak of Cao Cao, and Cao Cao arrives." This is equivalent to the English saying, "Speak of the devil."

The leading Chinese figure of the twentieth century, Mao Zedong, said that much of his understanding of military tactics until the late 1930s was influenced by *The Romance of the*

*Three Kingdoms*.[3] It was only when he assumed leadership of the Communist movement in the relative safety of northern China that he began to study the classical military writings. The book's extensive influence in popular culture makes this period extremely well known in Chinese history. Its translation into English also makes this one of the most popularly known periods of Chinese history in the Western world, and it is often compared to the romantic beliefs about Merlin, the knights of the Round Table, evil sorcerers, and courtly love during the Arthurian period.

HAN DYNASTY

The quick collapse of the Qin dynasty and introduction of the Han dynasty (which was itself replaced by the Three Kingdoms Period) represented the first instance of what historians call the dynastic cycle. Military victory by the founder of the dynasty gave him claim to the Mandate of Heaven. With a claim to the mandate, the various independent warlords and civil servants started to exhibit a bandwagon effect. Under a win-win situation, the various warlords, leaders of war bands, and civil servants joined the leading contender for the throne, kept their political positions and bases of power, or were promoted to important civil service posts. The new emperor often ruled with vigor and consolidated his political strength. As a leader who gained power through military strength, he possessed the political and military skill to subdue foreign enemies and rein in regional Chinese leaders. The military strength helped secure trade routes and the proper collection of taxes. Eventually, the expansion of borders and opulence of the court led to an excessive budget. Military commanders needed to be paid, troops had to be raised and supported, and borders needed to be defended. The emperors usually became less vigorous, the court descended into petty infighting, and local leaders exercised more power, such as diverting taxes to themselves. Central control eventually became impotent, canals and roads were left unrepaired, banditry increased, heavenly signs were interpreted by civil servants as "inauspicious omens," regional garrison commanders estab-

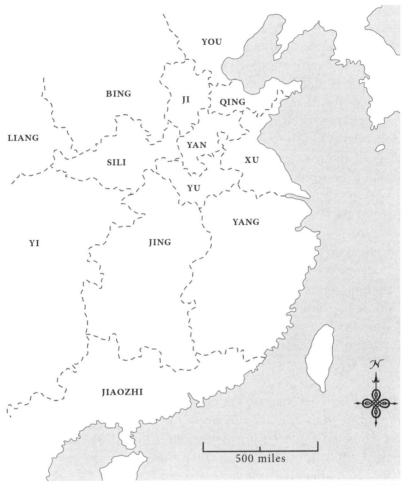

The Han Dynasty, 189. The later Three Kingdoms consisted of Wei, which went east to west along the Yellow River and provinces of Xu, Yu, Sili, and Liang; Wu, consisting of the three southeast provinces based on the Middle and Lower Yangtze; and Shu, in the southwest province of Yi, roughly centered in the Sichuan Basin.

lished their own bases of power, barbarians invaded, and local leaders revolted and contended for military supremacy and the claim to the Mandate of Heaven. Eventually one of them won. The regional warlords and civil servants rallied to the winner, and the cycle continued.

The division of Chinese dynasties isn't always accurate or the best way to divide history. Many long-term cultural trends transcended a specific dynasty. Many aspects of Chinese culture, such as the importance of the Seven Military Classics, or the spread of Buddhism, occurred independently of any one dynasty. Many of the dynasties were built slowly and incrementally. During periods of division, such as the Five Dynasties and Ten Kingdoms period of the early tenth century, the amount of time that elapsed from when a ruler proclaimed a dynasty to when his military and political victories actually secured his rule are too vast to point to a specific inception date of a dynasty. There were pivotal battles, such as those at Red Cliffs, that ended aspirations of would-be emperors, and other battles that induced a bandwagon effect, but the founding of a dynasty or its fall have somewhat arbitrary dates that obscure long-term trends surrounding negotiations between central and local powers. That said, it is useful to identify trends and developments during a particular dynasty. And it is an especially useful categorization for beginning students of Chinese history.

The founder of the Han dynasty started out as a rebel general against the remnants of the Qin dynasty. The leaders of the Han quickly asserted their power against the warlords who had submitted to their rule. For example, when an original ally died, the emperor replaced him with one of his close relatives. The naked application of Legalism (see below) by the previous dynasty had alienated many people, so Emperor Gaozu (d. 195 BC) cautiously asserted power and melded Legalism and Confucianism into its imperial form. He made punishments less severe and lowered taxes. But he did keep many of the tenets of Legalism and imperial Confucianism, which helped him rule.

ISMS: LEGALISM, CONFUCIANISM

The Chinese used *tian* as the word for sky or god that is often interpreted in later writings as heaven. During the Shang dynasty, the character started as *da*, or large man. Early priests added a horizontal line on their oracle bones, which meant extra-large man or king of kings. Shang Chinese believed in a supreme deity above that ruled over the earth but also lower deities such as the sun, moon, wind, and ancestors. The Shang king sacrificed to his ancestors so they could intervene on his behalf with the deity above. Worship in early China centered on the movement of the stars. The Chinese interpreted celestial events as omens from the gods. Later Chinese people stopped seeing deity in human form but instead thought of heaven as a force.

Several hundred years of constant fighting during the Warring States period whittled the states down to several of the strongest. One of these, the Qin, adopted a series of measures that granted them enough strength to unify China under their rule. One of the most import reforms of the Qin was the adoption of a series of rewards and punishments. These formed the basis of Legalism.

The leading Legalists, Han Feizi (d. 233 BC) and Li Si (d. 208 BC), argued that human nature is inherently selfish. Humans like comfort and rewards and dislike punishments and pain. Like the hypothetical youth in the first epigraph of this chapter, humans don't respond to the love of their parents but to the soldiers of a magistrate looking to execute the law. Legalists felt that true peace required a united country and strong state. So the state instituted severe punishments associated with breaking its laws, but it also included inducements for bravery in battle, loyalty, diligence, and frugal living. In one famous example of this principle from the sixteenth century, the famous general Li Rusong led his men from the front of the battle (earning a reward for bravery from the emperor), shot a man who had abandoned his position (the punishment), and promised a hefty bonus to the first man to scale the wall of their target city (the reward). The rewards extended to the lowliest peasant and the punishments to the highest official, which, according to Legalist thinkers, would lead to a stable realm from top to bottom.

In 221 BC, the armies of Shi Huangdi (256–210 BC) unified China, established control over areas as far south as modern-day Vietnam, and extended his influence into the steppes to the north. To help him control the barbarians he built a large wall. This is not the Great Wall seen today, which was built in the late Ming dynasty (sixteenth century), but it was over one thousand miles long and required vast amounts of labor. As many as one million people died building this wall. The emperor built roads and centrally controlled the collection of taxes. He standardized the writing of the language. He also collected and burned books from rival schools of thought within Confucianism. Some Confucian historians say that he had scholars who disagreed with him buried alive. The emperor had so much power that he was buried with an army of almost eight thousand life-size terracotta warriors to reflect his status when he died. Some of his measures, while unifying for China in the long term, generated incredible amounts of anger and resistance from court officials, the people, and local elites. After his death, the empire quickly disintegrated and was reformed, with the name of the Han dynasty.

The rulers of the Han dynasty combined the tenets of Legalism with a form of Confucianism. This kept much of the potency inherent in Legalism but made it much more acceptable to the masses. As a personal philosophy, Confucianism stressed proper forms of behavior (*li*) relative to one's position. The ruler ruled, the subject was a subject, the father a father, and the son a son. If everyone did their duty as required by heaven, it would form an unbroken chain of harmony, from the daughter of the lowliest peasant all the way up to the emperor.

While Confucianism often interacted with the political sphere, Daoism often affected people's private lives. The beliefs derive from the *Tao Te Ching* written by Laozi (c. sixth century BC). "Dao" simply means way. Many Westerners add "the" in front of it, but that often distorts the nature of "way." Way is the creator of the universe, sustainer of the universe, and the process, flux, or (as you might guess) way of the universe. Humankind's duty is to stay in harmony with that process. The yin-yang symbol represented this goal. It showed two perfectly harmonized halves. Ying and yang are opposites of one another but interact and produce harmony within a greater whole, and together they form one dynamic system. This notion overlapped with Confucianism, since people who acted properly had power flow to them. A sage, or one who acts in accordance with Daoist principles, can "do without doing" or affect people and events through the power of his moral lifestyle. A person should seek to become a true sage by regaining or returning to an original simplicity. The Daoists sometimes referred to this by saying a person must "return to being the uncarved block," or "return to being a babe." Politically, this meant that a ruler must not have too many laws or officials, since government can become oppressive from its own weight.

POWER AND CULTURE

The Han government had the military power and political cache to protect the Silk Road and establish a monopoly on salt. Both of these generated huge amounts of revenue. The Silk Road consisted of a connection of trading routes and cities that stretched from China to Rome. The items traded included silk, metalwork, and jewels from the Chinese, who imported horses, cattle, sheep, and jade from their neighbors on the steppe and glass and gold from Rome.

While not many archaeological finds go this far back in China, poets described the majesty of the capital city at Luoyang: massive walls, huge watchtowers, open courtyards, tiled gateways, broad boulevards, and the astounding size of the population. In fact, in later periods, when Marco Polo reported what he witnessed in China, it was so astounding to the Europeans that they thought he was exaggerating or lying.

Besides poets' capturing the majesty of the dynasty, archaeologists have recovered many fundamental Confucian texts dating to this period. In one of the many acts that prompted a backlash to his reign, the Qing emperor had ordered the confiscation and burning of many of the texts. But many leading families had hidden bamboo scripts in their walls or reproduced them from memory. In roughly 100 AD, Chinese scholars and bureaucrats created the first dictionary. On top of the standardized script, this helped bridge the gap between northern and southern dialects; it also created a standard for language that many other cultures emulated. The significance of this is similar to the invention of Arabic numerals, which allowed for the practice of mathematics across cultures through the ages. With the aid in writing, China also developed a tradition of writing histories. Sima Qian (d. 85 BC) wrote the *Historical Records*, which consisted of 130 chapters and 700,000 characters but also included what modern historians call primary sources.

CONCLUSION

Scholars still dispute the exact location of the Battle of Red Cliffs. But it represented a moment in time that has been highly influential in Chinese history. Cao Cao's rapid ascent and swift defeat crystallizes the romantic attraction to this age. The rise and fall of the Han dynasty illustrates the beginning of the disputed but still useful dynastic cycle and illustrates important cultural principles that formed ruling ideologies and guides on behavior. Chapter 3 will illustrate how these ruling ideologies and moral beliefs shaped the battlefield and conduct of Chinese wars.

3

# THE BATTLE FOR LUOYANG IN THE WAR OF THE EIGHT PRINCES

## 302–305

> By the [end of the war], trouble and disturbances were very widespread. . . . [M]any suffered from hunger and poverty. People were sold [as slaves]. Vagrants became countless. In the [provinces around the capital], there was a plague of locusts. . . . Virulent disease accompanied the famine. Also the people were murdered by bandits. Their rivers were filled with floating corpses; bleached bones covered the fields. . . . There was much cannibalism. Famine and pestilence came hand in hand.
> —*History of the Jin Dynasty*

THE CIVIL WAR AMONG THE SIMA CLAN that ruled the Jin dynasty in the early fourth century had raged for years. But there was a chance of peace—all the rival ruler called for was the head of Zhang Fang. The skilled general Zhang Fang scoffed at the idea and thought a military victory was at hand. He urged an attack and told his prince that their territory was rich and their troops strong and they were poised to once again descend on the capital. Other officials advised the potential ruler, Sima Yong, that Zhang was cruel and violent, and his behavior would lead to defeat.

They had a significant point. The fight for control of the empire centered on the capital of Luoyang and personal control over the figurehead emperor Huidi (Sima Zhong). Several years before that pivotal meeting in late 303, Zhang put the city under siege. He cut off the city's water supply and the city had to mobilize women and slaves to grind wheat by hand. The grain itself ran low, and prices skyrocketed. Even slaves were mobilized in defense of the city, but Zhang stormed the gates with his elite force. With fighting in the streets, the "arrows fell like fire," and flames lit the sky. In the seesaw fight for control of the capital, Zhang personally stormed the palace and seized the emperor. When the surrounded soldiers realized how few invading troops there were, they wanted to restore Sima Yi, the emperor's regent, but Zhang burned him to death.

The threats to Luoyang were not over. Taking the city was the easy part; ruling from it with a swarm of Sima contenders who wanted to also storm the capital and take control was much tougher. The original leaders who fought the war held military commands in key territories that led to the capital. During the war, and particularly this phase of it, those military leaders often returned to their centers of strength, but they could easily swoop down to harass those trying to rule in the capital. In fall 304, Zhang had to march against another contender advancing on the city. Zhang faced a food shortage as well and seized over ten thousand slave women. On the way west to meet the most recent challenge to his ruler's claim, he killed the slaves, minced them with meat, and fed them to his soldiers. After his victory and more machinations, he again sped back to the capital with crack troops and again seized and executed the next usurper, Sima Tan. A rival force then tried to smuggle the next figurehead emperor back into the capital, which would grant him legitimacy. In response, Zhang Fang sped from his protected valley to the west of the capital and captured them at their crossing of the Yellow River. This time Zhang's army returned to the capital and plundered it for months. They smashed cultural buildings, raped women, and seized whatever wealth they could for themselves. After several years of fighting Zhang's prince, Sima Yong still had not obtained sole control of the country.

By 307, Sima Yong arrived at a pivotal decision point between fighting on with his effective general or killing Zhang and sending his severed head as the opening gesture of peace talks with his distant cousin Sima Yue. Sima Yong chose the latter, and Sima Yue accepted the head—but he kept fighting. The war raged for several more years, but the damage to Luoyang was already massive. Contemporary and later Chinese historians recorded that the bones had been picked from the dynasty. Famine, slavery, cannibalism, and desolation reduced what was once a city that rivaled Rome in size and glory to no more than a few hundred shacks housing dying refugees.

The War of the Eight Princes is a vastly understudied conflict in Chinese history.[1] It doesn't have the allure of *The Romance of the Three Kingdoms*, and it is a one- or two-generation exception during a long period of disunion. But the same cultural values that informed the rise of the Han dynasty and later periods of military conflict were present during this period. The pivotal concepts about this period included the moral power of the Mandate of Heaven, the economic stagnation of war, the decentralization of power, the political and military art of the period, and the duration, intensity, and casualties of the conflict.

### THE FALL OF THE JIN DYNASTY

The War of the Eight Princes ended the short-lived (Western) Jin dynasty. This conflict is often overshadowed by the Han dynasty and the Three Kingdoms period (see chapter 2). Even dedicated sinologists have trouble following the kaleidoscope of various usurpers and their machinations in the War of the Eight Princes. After the Three Kingdoms period, Sima Yan united China and proclaimed the beginning of the Jin dynasty in the late third century. Sima Yan placed his relatives in strong military commands surrounding Luoyang on the Yellow River. As is typically the case in Chinese history, however, commanders capable enough to protect the frontier were also powerful enough to assert their will against the emperor. It took a strong emperor at the center to hold these ambitious commanders in check.

Upon the death of Sima Yan in 290, his mentally feeble son, Sima Zhong, assumed the throne as emperor Huidi. His wife, Empress Jia, suppressed, executed, or ran off members of the Sima clan and effectively ruled until 300. After the murder of Sima Yu, the various princes stationed along the periphery asserted their will in favor of the imperial (Sima) clan. Until this point, the various political machinations had been undertaken behind the façade of imperial authority. The empress signed an edict in the name of her feeble husband and then executed or exiled the various "traitors" to the empire. Two princes, Sima Yun and Sima Lun, violently seized power in the capital. Their naked use of power without an edict led to a violent plunge into chaos, and they forced the empress to commit suicide. Members of the Sima clan justified their actions based on assertions of military power and not imperial authority.

Less than a year after the princes' coup, Sima Lun killed Sima Yun and abandoned all pretense of ruling through his feeble cousin Sima Zhong (Huidi), and declared himself emperor. But this caused the former emperor's younger brothers—Sima Ying, Sima Yong, and an area commander, Sima Jiong—to attack from their surrounding commands. They defeated Sima Lun and restored their brother Sima Zhong (Huidi) to the throne. With the unremitting carnage among the princes in their struggles for power, by May 302, no clear heirs remained to the (recently restored) Jin emperor.

Sima Ying hoped for the nomination and resented the dominant position taken by the more distant relative Sima Jiong, while Sima Yong from the west also sought a role. In complex intrigue during the last days of the Chinese year heading into 303, Sima Ying and Sima Yong involved Sima Yi in their rivalry with Sima Jiong, but when Sima Jiong sought to destroy Sima Yi, Sima Yi turned the tables on him and took his place at the head of government.

After heavy fighting, Sima Yi defeated Sima Ying's forces and held off another army from Sima Yong, commanded by the vigorous, if violent and cruel, General Zhang Fang. However, Sima Yi was betrayed by his own soldiers, under the influence of Sima Yue. In 304, Sima Yue had Sima Yi imprisoned, but before the latter could be restored as regent, General Zhang, who served Sima Yong, burned him at the stake, but Yue continued his efforts to gain control over the emperor. Sima Yue's enemy, Sima Yong, tried to appease him by offering the head of his general. Sima Yue accepted the head but continued the fight to gain control of the government. He accomplished his design in 307.

The war gutted the strength of the Jin dynasty and marked the effective end of its rule in northern China. Sima Yue's victory ended the civil war, but the country was in a state of complete exhaustion. The Sima clan retained their positions but their extensive use of treachery, murder, and war—each person doing so in the name of the imperial family—left the legitimacy of the government in tatters and the army a shell of its former size and effectiveness.

## MORAL BELIEFS

The concept of the Mandate of Heaven, discussed earlier, granted the ruler legitimacy in the eyes of the people and helped secure his right to rule. This affected the War of the Eight Princes in at least three distinct ways. First, Empress Jia ruled through the command of her husband Sima Zhong (Huidi). She did not rule directly, but due to the Mandate of Heaven at least made it appear that everything was done by the emperor. Even with this façade, she had to tread carefully. When she killed the crown prince and his mother, it caused outrage among the population and gave her opponents the opening they needed.

One of her opponents, Sima Lun, could not completely capitalize on his victories due to the Mandate of Heaven. The people considered Sima Lun avaricious and false as well as simple and stupid. Once Sima Lun's alliance with Sima Yun and Sima Jiong was successful, he couldn't be the lead figure in the alliance, despite his key leadership role. Because Sima Lun was not trusted, Sima Yun was given an important command of capital troops to counter Sima Lun, as the ministers hoped his "resolute" character would offset Sima Lun's "improper ambitions." (Although Sima Lun later murdered Sima Yun to seize sole control.) The title of crown prince went to one of the emperor's grandsons. The machinations of the empire were done behind a veil of righteousness and duty, but it simply added several more layers of intrigue to maneuvering in the capital.

Finally, the Mandate of Heaven affected the power base of would-be rulers. Contemporary Chinese historians recorded that Sima Jiong shared many of the proclivities of the last emperors who had forfeited rule. He supposedly held lavish banquets in the capital and threw extravagant parties while ignoring the advice of his ministers to restore order to the realm. His generals called him a "rat that looks both ways," which implied that he was hesitant and indecisive. By 304, Sima Yi was under siege in Luoyang from several different armies and rival threats, including Zhang Fang. With the threat of famine hanging over his head, Sima Yi kept the emperor Huidi (Sima Zhong) at his side wherever he went, which ensured the loyalty of his soldiers. And the attempt of his followers to undo their surrender to Zhang and restore the emperor resulted in Zhang's executing Sima Yi. The Mandate of Heaven helped the emperor rule and inspired soldiers, but it could also place a ruler under the burden of being a good emperor and pose such a threat that it ensured a would-be ruler's demise.

### ECONOMIC STAGNATION AND LOCAL STRONGMEN

Economic stagnation resulted from, and contributed to, the loss of a rulers' legitimacy. The Jin dynasty was only a recent victor from the civil war that had lasted since the end of the Han dynasty a hundred years before. But this empire was far from a faithful re-creation of the Han dynasty. Centralized power was weak, and the vigorous monetary economy had stagnated. The lack of national trade allowed the local strongmen to leverage their power against an increasingly isolated capital. They could embargo the capital and confiscate taxes for their own use. Plus, the prosperity of the local populace was often intimately connected with the legitimacy of the central ruler.

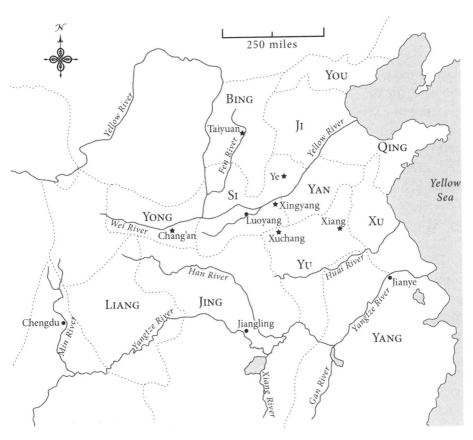

Jin military commands in the early fourth century. The commands are marked with stars and surround the capital of Luoyang. Sima Yong was based at Chang'an. (Xingyang should not be confused with Xiangyang; see chapter 7.)

The bad and good emperor dichotomy described previously applies here. Chief among these "good" practices were low taxes and the promotion of fruitful trade. Writers in the Seven Military Classics emphasized the ideas that as a good father, the ruler had to promote policies that benefited his people. So the economic embargo by regional leaders against the central government attacked not only his coffers but also his legitimacy. This was only compounded by the inability of the central government to ensure fair collection of taxes in its provinces.

All this resulted in a death spiral, as the government needed more money and soldiers to maintain power. So it levied more taxes in the areas still under its control, which led to the rise of disaffected groups. That in turn led to a decreasing tax base and the need for yet more confiscatory measures. This inspired a reassessment of the people's and the major leaders' loyalty to the emperor and central government, and it gave local strongmen and regional leaders the chance to offer a relatively easier burden, present just as a strong a case of having the Mandate of Heaven, and thus gain enough power to contend for the throne. This shows that the Chinese ruling ideology could be influenced by economic concerns and turn into powerful motivations and excuses for defying or trying to seize power.

These princes could use their economic power to keep the capital Luoyang in a general state of weakness economically and politically. But the moral significance associated with ruling the capital and the symbolic mandate it gave made its capture necessary. That is why so much of the fighting centered on Luoyang. Flush with troops and funds, the rival princes could move against the capital using the pivotal passes and rivers they were assigned to guard (such as Zhang Fang discussed in the opening of the chapter). In defeat, they could lick their wounds on the periphery until the balance of power between the other contenders presented an opening. Since they were assigned to guard pivotal passes and avenues of approach to the capital, they could also easily defend these approaches from forces sent from the capital. For example, a contender for the throne was defeated at the Battle of Tangyin. During this defeat, however, the contender managed to wound Emperor Huidi (Sima Zhong) with an arrow, and a few weeks later, another contender took advantage of the weakness in the center due to the emperor's state and came south against the capital.

POLITICAL AND MILITARY ART

Clausewitz famously and correctly described war as "politics by other means." This revolutionary activity includes striking at an enemies' Mandate of Heaven through economic warfare and performing the proper religious rituals in the capital. It also included using things like bribes, gifts, and even the temptations of wine and women to encourage them to indulge in their base practices and abandon the hard work of keeping the Mandate of Heaven and governing the kingdom. Other times rulers and would-be rulers used behind-the-scenes machinations and even assassinations to keep or gain power.

These techniques were seen repeatedly in the War of the Eight Princes. Empress Jia often invented charges with which to capture and execute potential rivals to the throne. Emperor Zhong was manipulated by no less than three other members of the Sima clan. Palace intrigue resulted in the execution of others. Once the façade of imperial authority faded, the rivals took their issues to the battlefields. Yet they still engaged in prebattle machinations, such as respectively offering and ignoring the severed heads of rival generals.

The political intrigues translated to the battlefield were no less sanguine or complicated. We can fruitfully use the example of General Zhang Fang, the leading general for Sima Yong, one of the eight princes, who led his troops with energy and vigor. Early in the war, Zhang Fang led a surprise attack on enemy forces. A short time later, he led a successful and daring night operation to supply his army. Later in the war, he argued for a decisive military attack using the language of classic Chinese theorists. Subsequent historians blamed his "cruel and violent" behavior as one of the sources for China's endemic conflict. Finally, rival leaders collaborated to murder Zhang Fang, then sent his head as part of a peace offering to a rival leader, who kept the head and continued fighting.

Zhang Fang's career during the War of the Eight Princes calls attention to the nature of military practice. This included heavy use of stratagem and ruses to psychologically undo opponents. Military practice was also intimately linked to contemporary political strife and subsequent moralizing from historians.

DURATION, INTENSITY, AND CASUALTIES

The War of the Eight Princes lasted roughly sixteen years, with numerous changes in rulers and shifting alliances. The princes of the Jin dynasty laid waste to the rival cities. The citizens in and around the capital city of Luoyang were almost continuously looted, raided, starved, eaten, conscripted, and attacked by Chinese and barbarian forces, until one of the largest cities of the third century world and most prosperous regions was desolate. Luoyang had an estimated six hundred thousand residents and its army may have had as many as seven hundred thousand soldiers at the start of the war, but the death rate was so high, it would be two centuries before its population reached prewar numbers.

While some may dispute the ability of premodern forces to kill large numbers of people, the raids, civilian losses, depredations, and lengthy, intense battles, combined with internecine political conflict, make the large numbers of deaths recorded in ancient texts entirely plausible. Additionally, there is evidence that there is no need for a special category of battles from "other" cultures separate from a distinctive "Western way of war." Scholars such as Victor Davis Hanson have argued that there is a distinctive and preferred method of fighting in the West that contrasts with the war-making practices of "others." A central component of this is a preference for shock battle. This is a battle that features a direct clash of arms between two opposing forces that essentially line up and charge at each other, in contrast with battle mainly decided by hit-and-run tactics and evasion. Starting with the Greek hoplites fighting short, decisive battles, then moving to the checkerboard formation of Roman legions, and the discipline of British Redcoats, scholars argue that this form of fighting has continued to the present. At least when it comes to shock battle, I join other scholars such as John Lynn and Kenneth Swope, who argue that the number of battles from non-Western cultures that feature direct clashes of armies undermine that part of the Western-way-of-war thesis.[2]

CONCLUSION

The War of the Eight Princes revealed numerous connections between Chinese thought about and practice of warfare: the impact of the Mandate of Heaven on the conduct of and pressures on political leaders; the use of economic power to disrupt trade so that it could be interpreted as a curse or loss of divine favor; a multitude of related claimants to the throne and the intrigues that ensued; regional power bases with control of the capital often serving as a catalyst for conflict; political ruses and a constant appeal to divine favor to justify war; reliance on prebattle ruses, and the sanguine results of the war in terms of duration, intensity, casualties, and preference for shock battle. The next battle features even larger numbers of deaths in one of the most decisive battles in Chinese history.

# 4

# THE BATTLE OF FEI RIVER

## 383

During the Taiyuan period of the Qin dynasty a fisherman . . . once rowed upstream, unmindful of the distance he had gone, when he suddenly came to a grove of peach trees in bloom. For several hundred paces on both banks of the stream there was no other kind of tree. The wild flowers growing under them were fresh and lovely, and fallen petals covered the ground—it made a great impression on the fisherman. He went on for a way with the idea of finding out how far the grove extended. It came to an end at the foot of a mountain whence issued the spring that supplied the stream. There was a small opening in the mountain and it seemed as though light was coming through it. The fisherman left his boat and entered the cave, which at first was extremely narrow, barely admitting his body; after a few dozen steps it suddenly opened out onto a broad and level plain where well built houses were surrounded by rich fields and pretty ponds. Mulberry, bamboo and other trees and plants grew there, and crisscross paths skirted the fields. . . . Men and women were coming and going about their work in the fields. The clothes they wore were like those of ordinary people. Old men and boys were carefree and happy.

When they caught sight of the fisherman, they asked in surprise how he had got there. The fisherman told the whole story, and was invited to go to their house, where he was served wine while they killed a chicken for a feast. When the other villagers heard about the fisherman's arrival they all came to pay him a visit. They told him that their ancestors had fled the disorders of the [earlier] times and, having taken refuge here with wives and children and neighbors, had never ventured out again; consequently they had lost all contact with the outside world. They asked what the present ruling dynasty was, for they had never heard of the Han, let alone the Wei and the Qin. They sighed unhappily as the fisherman enumerated the dynasties one by one and recounted the vicissitudes of each. . . . He stayed several days. As he was about to go away the people said, "There's no need to mention our existence to outsiders."

—Tao Qian, *The Peach Blossom Fountain*

If the enemy is forging a river to advance, do not confront them in the water. When half their forces have crossed, it will be advantageous to strike them. If you want to engage the enemy in battle, do not array your forces near the river to confront the invader but look for tenable ground and occupy the heights. . . . This is the way to deploy the army where there are rivers.

—Sunzi, *The Art of War*

THE BANDWAGON EFFECT in Chinese history—disparate groups joining to back a leading contender for power— might appear to be an endless cycle, but each would-be dynasty had its own unique story in its rise to power. After the collapse of the Jin dynasty and the resulting period of disunion, the Former Qin dynasty had one of the strongest claims to the throne. The Jin had collapsed from civil war, rebellion, and invasion. The Jin rulers fled south and consolidated their power around the Middle Yangtze. The remaining officials called that "skulking beyond the river." The leading politicians and heads of war bands remaining in the north fought for power; eventually one of them consolidated his power and then attempted to reunify the country by moving south. Normally this would have been the end of the familiar story about the rise of a new dynasty. But there were important differences that made this new attempt a failure at unifying the country and resulted in the longest period of disunion in Chinese history.

The main strength of northern Chinese armies was based in their cavalry. The geography, frequent contact with neighboring steppe tribes, and the new introduction of horse-riding equipment that facilitated the rise of heavy cavalry made it a particularly effective mode of combat in northern China. The Di tribe was a significant exception. It was usually subordinate to other tribes, many of which were allowed to settle in northern China in exchange for military service. The Di was the least nomadic of the tribes and largely focused on shepherding. As a result, it emphasized infantry-based armies. During the chaos after the fall of the Jin dynasty and the resulting period of disunion, the Di wanted to throw off the shackles of servitude and started its independence movement in the protected Wei River valley, just a short distance from the ancient capitals of Changan and Luoyang. Within several generations, its infantry-based army had deposed its neighbors and absorbed the rival soldiers. Following tradition, the Di made their submission easier by accepting the armies of surrendered generals, leaving their commanders in place, and even giving some of them selected positions in what historians call the Former Qin dynasty. (For our discussion we'll simply call it the Qin dynasty.)

The grandson of the founder of this Qin dynasty, Fu Jian (337–385), held control in northern China, while the remnants of the Jin dynasty still ruled in southern China. Fu Jian started south to capture the middle and lower Yangtze region. He besieged the key fortress at Xingyang, which his forces captured in 379. At the same time, his forces moved against the eastern flank of the dynasty. They captured strongholds that opened the door to the Jin capital at Jiangkang (modern-day Nanjing). A forceful Jin counterattack drove the invaders back across the Huai River. That river is about halfway between the Yangtze and Yellow Rivers and is generally considered the dividing point between northern and southern China.

Faced with a mild setback, Fu Jian ordered conscripts from

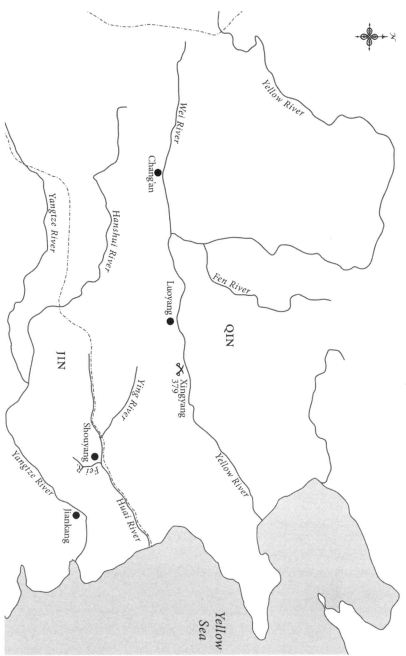

Qin and Jin territory in the late fourth century. The dotted line is the approximate boundary.

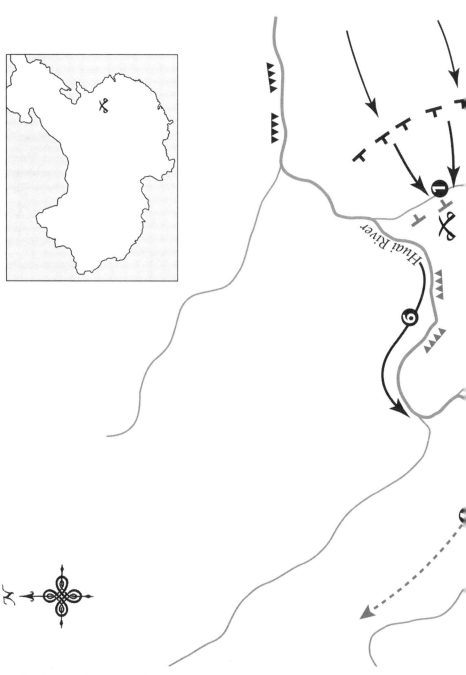

The Battle of Fei River, 383.

43

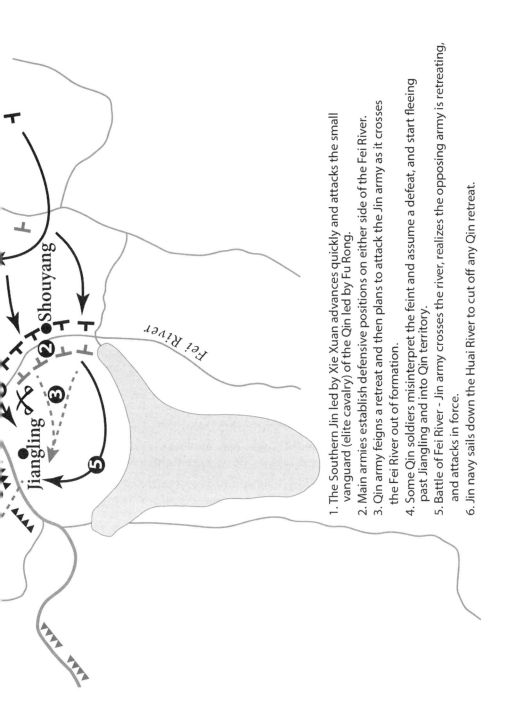

1. The Southern Jin led by Xie Xuan advances quickly and attacks the small vanguard (elite cavalry) of the Qin led by Fu Rong.

2. Main armies establish defensive positions on either side of the Fei River.

3. Qin army feigns a retreat and then plans to attack the Jin army as it crosses the Fei River out of formation.

4. Some Qin soldiers misinterpret the feint and assume a defeat, and start fleeing past Jiangling and into Qin territory.

5. Battle of Fei River – Jin army crosses the river, realizes the opposing army is retreating, and attacks in force.

6. Jin navy sails down the Huai River to cut off any Qin retreat.

all across his realm for the final assault. The numbers were said to be prodigious, with as many as nine hundred thousand soldiers. The plan in 383 was to advance in three columns, one in the west capturing the headwaters of the Yangtze in the Sichuan Basin. Another would advance in the east along the coastal plains. The main effort would advance from the city where the Qin forces had just been driven back.

The main Qin army advanced slowly along the river Fei, a north-flowing tributary of the Huai. But the fifty thousand Qin soldiers in the vanguard were pushed back by a daring night assault of five thousand Jin soldiers. The armies finally met and stared at each other across the river near the city of Shouyang. The Jin commander on the east side didn't want to assault a much larger force holding the opposite bank of the river. He asked the Qin commander, Fu Rong, to move back and allow his forces to cross the river. He contended that he wanted a quick resolution to the conflict instead of a lengthy siege.

Fu Rong's senior leaders advised against the idea. Their own army was bigger, but it was a collection of various tributary groups and poorly trained conscripts, which made the army rather unwieldy to maneuver. Even a small march might prove too unmanageable for the polyglot army. Holding the river bank and contesting any eventual crossing seemed like a stronger option to them, even if it resulted in a stalemate. Fu Rong dissented because he wanted to follow classic military theory and attack an army during a vulnerable river crossing. Without knowledge of the overall Qin plan, which was to fall back and allow the Jin to cross, but to then attack them in the process, individual soldiers interpreted the order to withdraw as a retreat and assumed another part of the army had been defeated. The rumor spread and the conscripts quickly panicked, trampling to death Fu Rong and his disciplined cadre of loyalists, who tried to corral the soldiers from fleeing.

The Jin soldiers successfully crossed the Fei and quickly pursued the panicked Qin army. Chinese chroniclers report that almost all of the nine hundred thousand Qin soldiers perished.

Those that weren't killed in combat, died because of hunger or exposure to the elements. If the battle didn't seem like a cataclysmic affair, the results certainly were. The Qin dynasty quickly collapsed into another series of competing warlords and states. China wasn't unified again until almost two hundred years later. The Battle of Fei River is considered one of the most decisive in Chinese history. The battle reveals the benefits of and drawbacks to the cultural idea of a unified China resulting from a would-be emperor's resounding victory or defeat, at which point many rival and unaligned officials, warlords, and generals supported the claimant or abandoned him. It tells us about the way Chinese historians recorded battles and how much modern readers should trust the numbers listed in ancient histories. Finally, it is another example that shows the difference between northern and southern China and how it usually resulted in separate northern and southern dynasties.

## BANDWAGON AND DIFFERENCES

The conspiring politicians and would-be rulers of the Qin Empire felt the crushing burdens of the Mandate of Heaven almost as often as they felt the benefits of it. The bandwagon effect for would-be rulers was one of the most decisive benefits of that mandate. The initial victories of a would-be emperor might have been based on little more than luck, or a limited and unique tactical situation that he exploited. For example, the Fu family had the benefit of being in a protected river valley not too distant from the pivotal centers of power. They could hold key mountain passes in a defensive position and selectively attack when their opponents were distracted or engaged. These initial victories based on luck or limited strategic situations encouraged rivals to defect. Defectors were induced by the fact that those who submitted received rather generous terms. Those who declared their loyalties to the new emperor often remained in command of their armies, and many even received important positions. This wasn't just generosity of the new emperor; he often still had limited control over his home territories, and this was a convenient negotiation of power under the guise of the mandate.

The new emperor had to staff a complex bureaucracy filled with Confucian scholars, manage the territory already under control, and continue to feed, equip, and pay the army he possessed, all while fending off rivals who resisted his power.

The compromise between the emperor and submitting warlords or Confucian officials allowed the emperor to strengthen his position, reduce the threats against him, and gain greater legitimacy. It also allowed the warlord, bandit chief, or army leader to keep power, have his position legitimized, and have a chance to amass greater wealth and power. The wins of the emperor produced a positive feedback loop. The initial winner received the submission of various warlords and leaders. This increased the ruler's tax base and the number of farmers he could call on to supply his army, and it made him look like a mandated ruler in the eyes of the Confucian officials who helped him govern and the people over whom he governed. But there were significant limits to this power. A single defeat could shatter an emperor's power. The rival generals still held their armies, so they could easily sense which way the wind was blowing and rebel, and because of the ideology surrounding the Mandate of Heaven, they could claim a powerful justification for their actions by arguing that the ruler had lost the mandate.

The conquest dynasties such as those from the Di were even more susceptible to this. Because they weren't ethnically Han (East Asians whose name derives from the ancient Han dynasty), they had to work harder to prove to the people—and most importantly, ethnically chauvinist officials and the elite—that they were sanctioned rulers of China. (This was a particularly difficult problem when a foreign dynasty had to respond to the western threat. See chapter 10.) Tribes like the Di didn't have skilled bureaucrats who could collect taxes, administer rituals of leadership, conduct a census that taxes households, and raise their armies. On top of this, the Di tribe had only gained power within recent memory. There were still many gaps to their rule. The various hilltop fortresses were only nominally loyal to the government. They still provided potential centers of opposition should the ruler falter and they shielded peasants from taxes and the imposition of corvee labor. This weakened the central government, as it couldn't pay its army and didn't have enough labor to build its own fortresses. The most potentially damaging effect on a would-be emperor's power was the tendency to relocate the population of defeated enemy states to areas around the capital. In times of severe chaos when central authority was weak or nonexistent, people often became more important than empty territory. By the time of the Battle of Fei River, there were over one hundred forty thousand households from the Xianbei and Qiang tribes stationed around the capital.

All of these factors meant that even though individuals like Fu Jian, Cao Cao, and Zhu Yangzhang (see chapter 8) had impressive records of military victory, charisma, and auras of power, their positions remained precarious. The defeat at Fei River quickly led to an unraveling of the empire, as the fortress chiefs, relocated people, and rival generals who still held command of their original armies all reasserted their will. The defections by fortress chiefs, relocated populations, and previously subdued but now deserting generals were especially harder to reverse in this case because many of the most loyal soldiers to the Qin dynasty were trampled and killed along with their leader, Fu Rong.

### NATURE OF CHINESE HISTORY

But the scope of defeat is perhaps exaggerated. The account of the battle comes from only one source, the history of Fu Jian. This was written by officials of the Jin dynasty trying desperately to sustain the legitimacy of the southern regime. The aura of legitimacy was only increased by portraying a catastrophic defeat of one of the Jin's enemies, and this became one of the biases that calls into question the accuracy of the account.[1] Despite the bias, it's tough to deny that the retreat from Fei River preceded a dramatic and sudden implosion of the Qin Empire.

This becomes an excellent example of the long-term trends that modern historians have noticed in Chinese history. These trends have particularly strong influence on Chinese military history. The Confucian scholars who were part of the ruling dynasty were responsible for writing history. Few of them had any military experience. In fact, there is a perception of Chinese culture as having a specific dichotomy that favors *wen* (or culture) or *wu* (or martial matters). There is even a Chinese proverb that states, "Good iron doesn't make good nails, and good men don't make good soldiers." *The Wuzi*, a writing within the Seven Military Classics, was actually suppressed by many Confucian officials because of its brutality. This means that the people writing the history were specifically opposed to the subjects and leaders in their writing.

That being said, the cultural bias is a bit overstated. Many generals throughout Chinese history had classical educations—some even wrote poetry and sponsored the arts—and many officials led rather successful armies. Despite the Confucian stereotype of the Chinese people as culturally averse to war and naturally coalescing, their empires formed and disintegrated because of war like any other culture. But there was still a perception at least, and many times a strong divide between *wen* and *wu* that persisted throughout Chinese history, and it did affect their writing on military matters.

The problems don't simply involve culturally minded historians who were sometimes actively hostile toward military matters. The sources they had to work with were sometimes sparse or wildly inaccurate. The Confucian historians often had to rely on announcements of victory. These were messages from frontier commanders to the general that included the dates, times, locations, and such things as the names of friendly commanders, their assignments, and troop dispositions. A recording of the actual course of the battle was lacking. Moreover, there aren't any announcements of defeat recorded, which suggests that the commanders were at best reluctant to send them and that they massaged the accounts (or commanded their scribes to do so when they couldn't write) in order to receive imperial favor. The accounts of the enemy dead were often wildly exaggerated and the friendly dead hardly reported. This seems done to make it seem as though their victories were miraculous.[2]

The other primary sources Confucian historians used were the accounts of conduct. These were even more self-serving, as they often acted like eulogies for dead commanders written by friends and relatives of the deceased. They often omitted unflattering information, distorted events to make the deceased look even more important, and presented many half-truths at best. The scribes compiling the accounts were often overworked and operating under tight deadlines, so they uncritically borrowed from these accounts and sometimes did wholesale insertions of these accounts into the records.

Finally, every history of the previous dynasty was commissioned by the current dynasty and written with a specific purpose. The writers had no interest in tactics, strategy, or the course of the battle unless they exemplified a teaching from a military classic. The Confucian scholars knew the great works, including the Seven Military Classics, and they believed that book learning mattered more than soldiering, so they made sure to include ideas from those writings to show it was the proper education of generals and application of principles that caused their victories. Because of the motivation of historians, the nature of the primary sources with which they worked, and the cultural bias of historians—though the last factor is somewhat overstated—there is a significant barrier to studying military history in China.

NUMBERS IN BATTLE

The final difficulty in military history includes the manipulation of the number of soldiers in battles. Here the record of Chinese battles largely matches those found in other cultures. Exaggerating the size of armies and numbers of the dead was often done for several reasons. Scribal error, the unreliability of eyewitness estimates, and the use of the wrong numbers to make a deliberate moral or political point were the primary factors. Ancient historians often wrote not to tell what happened but with a specific moral purpose. Hence, they didn't have the same scruples about bending facts to fit their story.

In Chinese history, this goes back to the Mandate of Heaven. Scribes, such as those writing the history of Fu Jian, were motivated to enhance the magnitude of the defeat of the stereotypical bad last emperor. This in turn enhanced the status of the current ruling dynasty (which conveniently commissioned the history in the first place.) According to the chronicle of Fu Jian, he mustered an estimated eight hundred seventy thousand troops to attack the eastern Jin dynasty in the late fourth century, and over seven hundred thousand of his soldiers died in the climactic battle. These numbers are vigorously disputed, but many Chinese sinologists point to the figures in the previous conflicts such as those in the War of the Eight Princes to show that Chinese dynasties could raise and destroy large armies in a short period. They also cite the many medieval Europeans who discounted Marco Polo's travels because of his seemingly unbelievably high numbers, yet his record was true and is now considered a vital primary source. The high numbers for this battle could also be true despite Western skepticism. But given the huge numbers and the scope of the defeat, it's likely the writers sponsored by the Jin dynasty inflated the size of the army opposing them and the magnitude of its defeat. Later Confucian scholars who finalized the book in the Tang dynasty (see chapter 5) probably massaged the numbers even further in an attempt to dissuade their current emperor from more military adventures.

Even though they were likely inflated or exaggerated, the numbers were still within the realm of possibility. While modern readers should have a healthy skepticism of numbers, the ancient Chinese could field and destroy large armies. The War of the Eight Princes decimated the western Jin dynasty in ancient China; scholars argue that the Jin army had seven hundred thousand soldiers at the start of the war. The battles from this civil war ranged across northern China for only about six years, and one ancient historian suggested that the capital province had only 1 percent of its population survive the conflict. Modern historians posit that the powers in the Warring States period from almost a thousand years earlier could possibly field up to half a million men for one campaign. Historians will likely never know what the true numbers were. There is good evidence that the numbers in the Battle of Fei River were wildly inflated (but just as strong evidence to say that those numbers were still possible) and that they were overstated because of political and cultural factors. Whatever the size of the army, the result of the battle is not in question.

## CHINESE GEOGRAPHY

The Battle of Fei River displayed a characteristic common in Chinese history. The northern Chinese forces had great difficulty in fighting in southern terrain, and vice versa. The rivers that the southerners used for logistics and travel became barriers to the northerners. These barriers necessitated Fu Rong's three-pronged attack at Fei River. One of the flanking armies was tasked with capturing the headwaters of the Yangtze River. Located in the Sichuan Valley, this would have allowed them to float a fleet down the river that could help supply and coordinate attacks with the land army.

China is roughly the same size as the United States or Europe (from the Ural Mountains to the west). That size brings diverse climates, crops, and lifestyles. The Yellow River flows west to east, and the area through which it flows is similar in climate and geography to the Midwest states of Indiana and Illinois. Unlike the Midwest, though, significant mountain ranges run both north-south and east-west that channeled armies through pivotal passes, reduced the arable land, and created a much higher population density at the time of the Battle of Fei River than the modern American Midwest. This area, in fact, is where ancient Chinese societies first formed and was home to historic capitals such as Luoyang and Changan, as well as the modern capital of Beijing. The armies here had large cavalry components suitable for fighting in the plains along the river and the steppe farther north of the Yellow River. The steppe also brought large contingents of nomadic forces as friend or foe (and sometimes both at the same time), from the Xiongnu tribes of the third century BC all the way to the Jurchens of the sixteenth century AD.

Farther south of the Yellow River region, the Yangtze River stretches east to west. The southern region dominated by the Yangtze also contains rather steep peaks, narrow river gorges, and little arable land. This resulted in the many carefully terraced hilltops that snake around the sides of hills filled with rice paddies. In great contrast to the northern regions with marked changes in weather between seasons, the southern climate is tropical, with numerous jungles and swamps. Tropical diseases often sapped the strength of northern armies operating in southern regions. (Remember the sickness that incapacitated Cao Cao, for example.)

The hills, swamps, mountains, and two major east-west rivers created a multitude of almost completely isolated geographic areas within China. Most of the future rulers of China started their careers in regions like the Sichuan Basin on the Upper Yangtze, the Middle and Lower regions, and the northern Yellow plain or from some of the main regions under consideration. When central Chinese authority weakened, many of the regions attained some semblance of independence. The southern realms had strong naval forces—trained marines used to operating in water, rivers, marshes, and storming boats—and strong infantry forces. The northern powers attempting to attack the south were usually at the end of their logistical limits on tributary rivers. This made it easier for southern forces to send a flanking attack. Cutting the logistical cord was often enough to weaken the armies to the point they had to withdraw.

Southern forces faced their own share of problems as well. Their navies excelled in the narrow rapids and gorges of the Yangtze but could not help them project power in the north. When their armies marched north, they faced the same logistical limits and susceptibility to flanking attacks as northern armies. They were dangerously lacking in cavalry. They had little need for cavalry forces in the south, little land in which to breed horses, and therefore limited experience with horsemanship. Tactically, southern cavalry was often mowed down by the charges of the north's heavy cavalry. The north often had to face dangerous and fast nomads, so they could easily outflank their southern partners with their own speedy cavalry. Many of the southern dynasties that expanded into the north were rump states that regrouped after losing their northern lands. The northern military families that supported the southern court would end up losing most of their lands and were thus far weaker and had far less access to the emperor in the south. An emperor from the south often lacked soldiers directly loyal to him, which meant that the more success a general had in regaining the north, the more that general became a threat to the court itself. Many of these successful generals swooped south along the Yangtze and established their own regimes by force. Finally, the southern elites did not want to send their forces so far away from their local bases of power, so the leaders of the south often faced numerous challenges prosecuting and controlling the war in the north.

CONCLUSION

As Fu Jian and many others found out, the southern territories were very hard to capture. Throughout Chinese history, from the Chin dynasty to the Three Kingdoms period to the Sui and Mongol invasions all the way to Chiang Kai-shek in the twentieth century, southern China could occasionally be a base of power for would-be rulers but was usually the last refuge of a dying dynasty. A single defeat could bring ruin to would-be emperors. Their power often rested upon the victory of their armies. It was negotiated with local rulers, such as the hilltop fortress chiefs in Fu Jian's day, but also various warlords and officials looking for a mandated ruler. They fought battles with armies of unknown size, which was likely exaggerated for effect, but could still be very large. China would face a long period of disunion, and it was the combination of effective military leadership and excellent use of naval forces that finally united the country under the Sui dynasty.

# 5

# THE BATTLE OF YAN ISLAND

## 589

Drunk-Land lies at I cannot say how many thousand li from the Middle Kingdom. Its soil is uncultivated, and has no boundary. It has no hills nor dangerous cliffs. The climate is equable. Nowhere is there either darkness or light, cold or heat. Customs are everywhere the same. There are no towns; the inhabitants live scattered about. They are very refined; they neither love, nor hate, nor rejoice, nor give way to anger. They inhale the breeze, and drink the dew; they do not eat of the five cereals. Happy in their rest, dignified in their movements, they mingle freely with birds, beasts, fishes, and crustaceans. They have no chariots, nor boats, nor weapons of any kind. . . . Under the Great Yü (2205 BC), laws were instituted, rites were numerous, and music was of varied kinds, so that for many generations there was no communication with Drunk-Land [until today]. . . . However, certain enlightened friends of mine often slipped across on the sly. The poet Tao Chien, and others, to the number of ten or a dozen, went off to Drunk-Land, disappeared there and never came back; they died there and were buried in its earth. They are known in the Middle Kingdom as the Wine Immortals. Ah me! How different are the customs of the people of Drunk-Land from those of the country of the mother of Fu Xi (3rd millennium B.C.) of old! How pure and peaceful they are! Well, I have been there myself, and therefore I have written this record.

—Wang Qi, *Drunk-Land*

Thus the victorious army is like a ton compared with an ounce, while the defeated army is like an ounce weighed against a ton! The combat of the victorious is like the sudden release of a pent up torrent down a thousand fathom gorge. This is the strategic disposition of force.

—Sunzi, *The Art of War*

IN 588, THE GENERALS OF THE SUI DYNASTY completed their massive fleet. The emperor chose one of his most talented and experienced generals, Yang Su (d. 606), to lead the flotilla. The construction at the headwaters of the Yangtze included what they called "five banner warships." These were massive ships with five decks that could transport up to eight hundred men per ship. The top deck was big enough to hold siege equipment such as trebuchets. The ship contained six, fifty-foot-long spiked booms that could be dropped onto opposing ships. If that didn't destroy them outright, it pinned them in position and allowed the eight hundred archers to rain arrows and fire arrows on the hapless vessel. Construction also included small Yellow Dragon-class ships that were faster and could hold about one hundred men.

The Sui dynasty had followed the time-honored Chinese tradition of rising to power in the north before organizing a significant naval campaign against the south, but it had several advantages over it predecessors.[1] First, it did a much better job of consolidating the north. The mixed Sino-Turkish elite that had developed over hundreds of years of conquest and intermarriage between foreigners from the steppe and ethnic Han had produced a vigorous set of leaders with the ethnic credentials to impress and enlist Confucian elites, and a long heritage of martial skill. The combination allowed the northern Zhou kingdom to absorb its neighbors and become the vigorous Sui dynasty.

It had also expanded a great deal into southern China. It didn't have to worry about supply lines extending from the Huai or Han Rivers, fortresses blocking their approaches to the Yangtze, or a tenuous supply line that could be cut. Yang Su was supervising the building of a fleet at the headwaters of the Yangtze itself, not far from the World War II capital in Chonqing. Other columns of troops (eight in total, three completely naval and a fourth that was mixed, totaling five hundred thousand men) could embark or ford the river from the northern bank of the Middle Yangtze.

By late autumn 588, Yang Su embarked with his flotilla. The overall strategy was to pin down the opposing naval forces using his fleet in the Upper Yangtze, which should allow troops near the Chen capital of Jiangking to cross the river and take the city. If the opposing fleet did not engage Yang's forces, then he could descend toward the east, make a flank attack on defending forces, and assist in taking the capital and deposing the rival emperor.

Yang Su had the advantage, but it wasn't a foregone conclusion that he would succeed. Larger forces than his had failed, and the south still had the advantages of terrain, in particular a nasty series of swift currents, narrow gorges, and strong fortresses that lined his approach to the capital.

The first resistance was a combination of two forts, several thousand men, and a large contingent of Green Dragon-class warships contesting the passage of Wolf Tail rapids. Yang Su feared being attacked from both directions if he advanced in daylight. It was dangerous, but he decided to advance through the narrow rapids at night and bypass the force. Historians report that he forced his men to bite on sticks to enforce noise discipline. In addition, he had landed two raiding parties north of the river forts.

The Chen forces didn't think Yang Su would try to negotiate the rapids in the dark with the risk of attack from the soldiers on alert. They were surprised, then, to be attacked from land and sea during the night. Yang's daring had paid off handsomely with a large haul of prisoners, and he continued down the river.

Yang faced the next challenge about twenty miles farther, where his opponent had laid three giant iron chains across the river. Yang couldn't bypass them, so he landed soldiers again, but this time on both sides of the river. They launched several costly frontal assaults before finally seizing the forts in a night attack. The chains were cut and the opposing fleet fled to the strong defensive position at Yan Island.

By this point Yang didn't see the need for subtlety. He placed his five banner ships in the front of his formation and charged down the river. Unlike Western navies, they didn't attempt to ram or board ships. The spiked boom of the warship destroyed dozens of craft, and the hundreds of archers on each ship killed many more soldiers. By this point, most of the defense leading to the enemy capital of Jiangkang had collapsed, and the city itself was close to falling. Over the course of the campaign, Yang destroyed dozens of ships, captured thousands of men, sent the remaining enemy fleeing, and shattered the defense of the entire western one-third of the Chen state.

The defending Chen dynasty had fewer soldiers, it is true, but their situation was compounded by weak defense measures. The infighting among Confucian officials paralyzed potential defensive policies, which meant the emperor ended up keeping most of the remaining navy around the capital. The exceptions were the fleet defeated by Yang Su.

The Sui commander opposite the capital also used a combination of ruses to advance unopposed. He hid his good ships and displayed decrepit hulks. He went on large game hunts near the river, ostensibly to feed his soldiers, but their real purpose was to condition the enemy to ignore large troop movements near the river. And he deliberately allowed the enemy to see through other ruses, which led the defending troops to relax further. When he did cross the river, he smashed the surprised enemy and advanced to Jiangkang unopposed by the Chen fleet, which was still harbored and paralyzed around the capital.

The final battle took place on the high ground east of the city. Again, the Chen dynasty had a good number of soldiers, but unwise deployment made it difficult for them to reinforce each other. One of the subcommanders for the Chen showed initiative, but when his force was repelled (using burned grass to con-

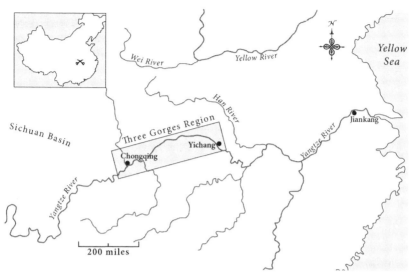

The Three Gorges region. The area within the box is enlarged in the map opposite. Jianking was the southern capital of the Chen dynasty (a short-lived southern successor to the Jin from the previous chapter). Chonqing is a pivotal city near the headwaters of the Yangtze where Yang Su of the Sui dynasty launched his attack. Yichang is located by the third and east-ern-most gorge. The Chen saw this area as their best location to mount a defense.

ceal the Sui redeployment of forces), the Chen army retreated in a general rout. The rival emperor was deposed, and many of the remaining units quickly submitted to the new dynasty.

The final outcome of this battle reveals many trends seen in Chinese history during the period of disunion. It showed the influence of western tribes on the culture of northern elites, the spread of Buddhism, the increasing importance of the south, and Chinese expansion at the expense of southern tribes.

## TRENDS IN THE PERIOD OF DISUNION

This victory in early 589 ended the Chinese period of disunion. This was the longest period of division from the start of imperial China in the second century BC until the last dynasty fell in 1911. While this time defies easy periodization and seems like an aberration, it produced many important trends in Chinese history.

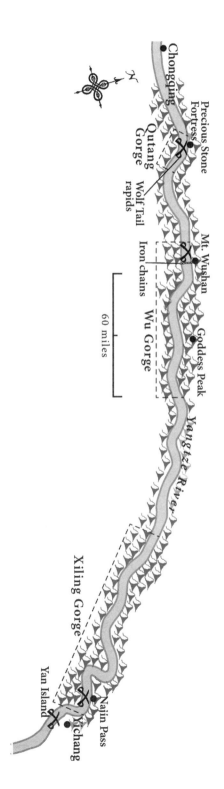

The Battle of Yan Island, 589.

These trends somewhat mirror what happened in western Europe with the fall of the Roman Empire. The West witnessed a merging of cultures between Germanic tribes and Roman settlers. This mixture created what medieval historians started to call Europe. A similar event happened in China, but Confucian historians, acutely aware of their privileged status in the Middle Kingdom, often argued that Chinese culture eventually conquered the barbarians. The new ruling elites of the barbarian kingdoms employed civilian bureaucrats to collect taxes and provide legitimacy for their rule. They intermarried with leading Chinese families and started to learn the Chinese script of their more sophisticated neighbors. At first this led to more division, as one part of the family became more like the Chinese in the capital while their relatives stayed in frontier garrisons along the steppe. The latter group married their own ethnicity, retained their language and customs, and kept their military skills honed. This contributed to the Chinese period of disunion, as they revolted against their seemingly decadent relatives in the capital. Over generations, there was a much stronger fusion between the western tribes and the Chinese. It came to be seen as ideal for a leader to have a strong foundation in Confucian classics but also a mastery of archery, horseback riding, and a robust grasp of strategy and statesmanship. Yang Jian, who became Emperor Wen when he founded the Sui dynasty, exemplified this trend. He led a coterie of strong generals like Yang Su who could unify China.

The introduction and influence of Buddhism was particularly pronounced in this period. Roughly contemporary with the founding of Christianity, missionaries spread Buddhism to China in the first century AD. Originally, the Chinese simply viewed it as a new strain of Daoism. Many early translators used Daoist terms to describe Buddhist concepts. With the collapse of the Han dynasty, the religion spread rapidly. It contained a doctrine of personal salvation with several routes to that goal. Like Confucianism, it contained high standards of personal ethics. It received continued inspiration from India, such as advanced meditative practices. Buddhism in India had started as a reform movement, but Chinese Buddhism combined with local religions. They used the meditative procedures of early Buddhism and believed it represented a Confucian form of self-improvement. Chinese Buddhism added a different strain of philosophy that combined a succession of Buddhas that formed a force similar to the Daoist concept of way. Socially, Buddhism demanded that heirs perform sacrifices to their ancestors. Chinese Buddhism required that first sons have families so the sons could fulfill the familial piety required by Confucianism, but they also believed this prevented "hungry ghosts," which represent unpleased spirits from Buddhist thought. And they encouraged second sons to become monks.

Daoism and Buddhism compared in some ways to Western religions. Their principles governed personal lives, brought comfort during chaotic periods filled with endemic war, and created potent political philosophies. During the period of Chinese disunion, many monks created large monasteries that provided oases of order. Much like their European counterparts, these Buddhist monks preserved ancient texts, administered law and order, delivered food to nearby peasants, provided basic medical services, and, in the case of some militant orders, formed armies. Vigorous emperors of the resurgent Tang (618–907) and Song (960–1279) dynasties often severely pruned these monasteries and confiscated or heavily taxed their lands. This was often the result of a monastery's material excess, interference in politics, and antagonism from warrior monks. As the religion of both the Chinese and the western tribes they associated with, Buddhism acted as a unifying force.

But the major Chinese belief systems differ from Western religions in important ways. They have no concept of a single God. Heaven is more a cosmic order, so Chinese religious leaders did not record theophanies (the appearance of a deity to a human) and did not form institutional churches. Thus, Chinese history does not contain the equivalents of such things as papal decrees or an investiture controversy, during which European leaders battled the pope for the right to ordain priests in their realms. Not having a concept of God decreased the duality between the spiritual and natural words seen in Western religions, in which heaven is above, earth below, and people in between. Chinese religions contained more thought comparable to the Greek philosophers. But even the Greeks were more speculative about societal issues and theology, while Chinese philosophies often commented on how religious principles applied to practical issues of righteous daily living and political concerns. Chinese emperors modified Confucianism to bolster the strength of imperial dynasties.

## EXPANSION INTO THE SOUTH

The campaigns of Yang Su focused on the Yangtze River. This had been an important center of Chinese strength since the Qin dynasty. But successive Chinese rulers held only isolated areas along the Middle and Lower Yangtze for much of that early period. Both Cao Cao and Fu Jian fought in this region to try to control the south. The territory along the river was often rough and jagged and meant that settlements consisted of isolated pockets of Han Chinese in between different ethnic groups who practiced economies other than farming. Farther from the river, the terrain became even more rugged. A distant central government almost always had difficulty controlling mountainous and rough terrain which is why in the nineteenth and twentieth centuries, for example, the Taiping Rebellion and Mao's insurgency both started in these remote regions. In this early period, the tribes around Chinese settlements were often fiercely independent or only nominally loyal to the emperors.

But the period of disunion changed these Chinese settlements in the south from islands to the dominant culture. The trickle of settlers from the north soon turned into a flood. The relatively flat land around the northern Yellow River made it much more difficult to find shelter or protection from threats. The same trends that prevented the easy conquest of the south by northern armies also made it rather attractive to settlers fleeing chaos in the north. Individuals, small groups, and more often entire households and towns under a mayor or provincial official relocated to the south. They formed defensible farming communities on the sides of mountains (using terraced rice fields). The southern empires often had a difficult time raising armies because southern elites jealously guarded their manpower. This created a quid pro quo whereby the southern emperor granted land in relatively unpopulated areas in exchange for registering part of or an entire community as military households. During the early periods, these military households were valuable members of the state. They received tax breaks on their land, since farming helped the military household supply its own food, and the excess could be sold to fund armor and weapons. In exchange, the government received a steady supply of soldiers, usually one male from each military house, and it didn't have to pay for feeding or equipping the soldiers. The government did forego the tax revenue on the lands of military households, but it didn't lose any money out of pocket, only future tax revenue from new families. As the dynasty declined, these households often became little more than slaves, with soldiers being forced to serve far into old age and scrambling to find replacements. They were often absorbed into the private armies of local landlords or, more often, considered servants of the state.

The new Chinese settlers ended up displacing original tribes in a process not too unlike American expansion in the West. (In fact, modern Chinese politicians often justify their occupation of Tibet using similar analogies.) Even as late as the twentieth century, there was sometimes a divide in provinces between the *hakka,* or old settlers who lived in the rough highlands on the economic, political, and geographic margins of society, and the new settlers who worked prosperous farms in lowlands near major centers of power, such as Nanchang in Jiangxi Province and who made up most of the political leadership and dominant families of the province. The ethnic, political, and economic isolation of the old settlers eking out a living in rough terrain made them prime recruits for Communist revolutionaries proclaiming economic reform.[2] Some of the tribesmen adopted an if-you-can't-beat-them-join-them attitude. For example, the five banner ships that led the attack at Yan Island had included thousands of archers from southern tribes. But most of the time, the frontier was the location of fierce friction between the original settlers and the new or guest settlers.

A combination of ethnic tension, raids, assaults, and the rebellion of southern elites losing privileges inspired a rather massive campaign by Yang Su. Yang's army ended up marching more than three hundred miles and fought more than seven hundred engagements throughout southern China. The army was so remote that it was out of contact with Sui officials for more than one hundred days. This campaign finally put the south under firm control, or at least as firm as ever.

CHINESE IMPERIALISM

Imperialism, combining racism, economic exploitation, and military superiority, is normally thought of as a Western wrongdoing committed against indigenous peoples. However, China, and by extension, other non-Western powers, are not unique victims of European racism, but had their own versions of imperialism and causes for it. China did face imperialism, but its weak state at the time wasn't necessarily a result of greedy foreign invaders. Chinese dynasties often had periods of expansion and collapse. During the early periods of a given dynasty, and particularly the Han and Tang, Chinese forces often controlled territory as far south as Hanoi, as far west as the Tarim basin in modern-day central Asia, and much of Korea. The Ming dynasty even sent large treasure fleets to much of Southeast Asia and even the east coast of Africa. (One theory posits those treasure fleets actually discovered America.)

The early Sui and Tang dynasties demonstrate this pattern. Yang Su conquered the southern tribes and imposed Chinese political power and cultural ideals as far south as modern-day Vietnam. A dominant facet of Chinese history and culture was the violent expansion and conquest of nonethnic Han people. In fact, the Chinese people called themselves Middle Kingdom because Chinese literati considered themselves a beacon of civilization and culture in Asia with barbarian kingdoms bordering them in every direction. The Chinese writing system, imperial style of government, and religion did spread to and inspire neighboring countries. Even their foreign policy was centered on a parent-child relationship whereby various powers had to approach them as a dutiful son showing the proper amount of filial piety.

The corollary to this is the idea that China had something special that enticed the greed of foreigners. During periods of weakness, the Chinese faced invasion. Because every adult male in nomadic societies could ride a horse and rode off to war, compared to a relatively small percentage of males in sedentary societies who were conscripted, nomadic groups often had prodigious militaries compared to their relatively small populations. Yet the nomadic lifestyle of grazing sheep and raising horses couldn't match the wealth and luxuries created in sedentary societies. The period of disunion shows this pattern most clearly as China faced invasions for three hundred years. But China built primitive versions of the Great Wall as far back as the Chin dynasty in the second century BC. It built a series of dikes and canals to prevent the invasion of Jurchen tribes during the eleventh century. And the sixteenth century Ming dynasty faced invasion and created the current version of the Great Wall. The invasions weren't simply foreigners eyeing China with "tiger like voracity,"[3] but a factor of two different kinds of societies living in close proximity to each other. As a sedentary people, the Chinese farmed, worked metal, and created silk garments. To put it simply, they had products that nomadic groups living on the steppes couldn't produce for themselves.

The Chinese used a variety of tactics to subdue the threats. During periods of strength, particularly the Tang dynasty under Li Shimin (ruling name Tang Taizong), they could use their elite heavy cavalry to pursue and destroy nomadic armies. Under weaker dynasties, the logistical requirements of infantry-based armies made the nomads practically untouchable once they retreated to the steppes and uncatchable when they disengaged from Chinese forces. Extensive military campaigns were adopted as far back as the early Han dynasty, but these were often inconclusive.[4] The Chinese rulers then set up trading outposts. This provided a way for the powers on the steppe to trade for the things they needed. The Chinese received warhorses and sometimes shipments of hides, or meat, from the herds they kept. During periods of greater Chinese weakness, they provided payments, often in lengths of silk, to the various tribes, from the Xiongnu to the Mongols. Or they offered marriage proposals under the guise of allowing the nomads to join the Heavenly Family led by the emperor. Even in periods of weakness, they couched the payments or offers of marriage in terms that still cast China as the Middle Kingdom and center of the world order. In short, the Chinese gave as well as they got. They often practiced a form of imperialism when strong and always exercised cultural influence, even in periods of weakness. During that weakness, they used ethnically chauvinistic reasons to justify their position.

CONCLUSION

Yang Su's fleet showed the importance of a navy in conquering southern China. It showed the strength of the Sui dynasty, as it succeeded where many others in the period of disunion had failed. The mix of Turkish nomads and ethnic Han produced a new martial vigor in northern leaders who could rule from the saddle. It also showed Chinese expansion into the south and provides much-needed context for the sometimes sad realities that accompany imperial expansion, and it pushes back on the idea that imperialistic expansion is unique to the West. It was the Tang dynasty and the subject of the next chapter that truly represented China's golden age and biggest expansion of power.

An iron sword, left, and two bronze swords and a bronze helmet from the Warring States period, 475–221 BC. Iron weapons used from horseback were important developments during this period. (*Gary Lee Todd*)

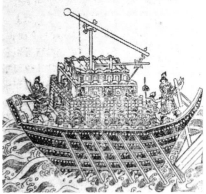

Song dynasty warships. Note the traction trebuchet mounted on top of the ship to the right. After the fall of their northern territories the Southern Song fleet protected the dynasty against the much larger Mongolian invasions, 1127–1279. (*Zhongguo bingshu jicheng; Chinese Siege Warfare by Liang Jieming*)

Chibitu (Red Cliff) by Wu Yuanzhi (detail). This is the earliest known painting of the location of the third century battle, and includes a rare example of semicursive calligraphy and art from the Jurchen dynasty that conquered the northern Song in the twelfth century. (*National Palace Museum, Taipei*)

Terracotta crossbowman, left. The first emperor of the Chin dynasty had himself buried with hundreds of life sized warriors. At the time of their burial they were incredibly colorful pieces of art. Right, Li Shimin (598–649). Ruling as Emperor Taizong, he is one of China's most accomplished and celebrated leaders. (*Camphora; National Palace Museum, Taipei*)

Tang dynasty cavalry statue. The Li family that established the Tang dynasty originated from a region in northeastern China. Years of intermarriage between ethnic Han and steppe tribes produced capable Chinese leaders with strong cavalry components in their armies. This helped the Tang spread Chinese influence across much of central Asia. (*Guillaume Jacquet*)

A wall painting of Northern Qi dynasty cavalry, c. 550–577. During the period of disunion (220–589) the northern Chinese realms relied upon fearsome heavy cavalry, while the southern Chinese relied upon naval forces and marines. (*Tomb of Lou Rui, Taiyuan*)

Mongols fighting the Chinese in the late thirteenth century. Despite the perception of the Mongols as a large horse army, their conquest of southern China relied on a mixed force of naval ships, infantry, and improved artillery. (*UKRMAP*)

The siege of Pyongyang, 1592–1593. An excellent example of classic Chinese water coloring that shows the chaos of battlefields during the early gunpowder era. (*Seventeenth century screen painting, Hizen-Nagoya Castle Museum*)

Battle of Zhengjiang, July 21, 1842, the last battle of the First Opium War. British soldiers disembarked, seized the city (including the west gate of the bridge shown above), and cut the vital Grand Canal to the capital of Beijing. The Manchu soldiers fought well and inflicted heavy casualties on the invading British. (*"West Gate of Ghing-Keang Foo," 1842, detail, Brown University Library*)

Regaining Jinling after the Taiping Rebellion (1851–1864). A religiously inspired conflict roughly contemporary with the American Civil War, the Taiping war resulted in millions of deaths, but demonstrated the continuing strength of the Qing dynasty and the need for them to reform their armies using gunpowder weapons. (*Wu Youru, c. 1886*)

Nanjing arsenal, built by Governor Li Hongzhang, in an 1872 photograph. One of the loyal and victorious generals from the Taiping Rebellion, Li was a major reformer in the late nineteenth century, though a major problem was the lack of standardized equipment and collaboration among reformers. (*John Thomson, in Historica, Yamagawa Shuppan*)

Mao Zedong, above left, and Jiang Jieshi (Chiang Kai Shek), right, two leading figures of twentieth century China. Their legacies continue to affect China and Taiwan today. Japanese soldiers entering the port of Ningbo, 1937, left. Naval landings south and north of Shanghai flanked Chinese forces fighting there and forced a Chinese withdraw towards Nanjing. Pill boxes in Changsha, bottom, during the heavy attacks of the Ichigo Offensive, 1944–1945. The fierce resistance from Chinese soldiers is often forgotten by the West. (*Hammerton/Gwynn, The Second Great War*)

# 6

# THE BATTLE OF HULAO

## 621

In the time of the accomplished Emperor Taizong, the illustrious and magnificent founder of the dynasty, among the enlightened and holy men who arrived was the Most-virtuous Olopun, from the country of Syria. Observing the azure clouds, he bore the true sacred books; beholding the direction of the winds, he braved difficulties and dangers. In the year of our Lord 635 he arrived at Changan; the Emperor sent his Prime Minister, Duke Fang Hiuenling; who, carrying the official staff to the west border, conducted his guest into the interior; the sacred books were translated in the imperial library, the sovereign investigated the subject in his private apartments; when becoming deeply impressed with the rectitude and truth of the religion, he gave special orders for its dissemination. . . .

Orders were then issued to the authorities to have a true portrait of the Emperor taken; when it was transferred to the wall of the church, the dazzling splendor of the celestial visage irradiated the illustrious portals. The sacred traces emitted a felicitous influence, and shed a perpetual splendor over the holy precincts. According to the Illustrated Memoir of the Western Regions, and the historical books of the Han and Wei dynasties, the kingdom of Syria reaches south to the Coral Sea; on the north it joins the Gem Mountains; on the west it extends toward the borders of the immortals and the flowery forests;

on the east it lies open to the violent winds and tideless waters. The country produces fire-proof cloth, life-restoring incense, bright moon-pearls, and night-luster gems. Brigands and robbers are unknown, but the people enjoy happiness and peace. None but Illustrious laws prevail; none but the virtuous are raised to sovereign power. The land is broad and ample, and its literary productions are perspicuous and clear.

—Christian Monument in Changan, 781

LIKE PREVIOUS DYNASTIES, the Sui lasted only a short time. The massive campaigns in Korea had taxed the resources of the state and led to revolt and rebellion, and in the chaos, the Li family emerged as one of the strong contenders to consolidate power. Li Shimin's father was Duke of Taiyun, in the pivotal Fen River valley north of the capital at Luoyang. His son Li Shimin put Wang Shicong under siege in the capital in 620. The latter sent a request to Dou Jiande for help. He was based in the plains surrounding the Yellow River to the east. They weren't the closest of friends, but they shared political interests that made them both want to fight Li. Dou knew that if Li captured the capital, Dou would be the next target. Only Li would have the additional surrendered soldiers of Wang, and the additional territory and prestige from capturing Luoyang. It would also increase Li's case for possessing the Mandate of Heaven. Finally, Dou hoped that after he defeated Li, he could be the one to absorb Wang's now-weakened regime.[1]

Li took a small force, no more than half of the fifty thousand at Luoyang, and went to defend the critical Hulao Pass to the east of Luoyang. The valley is described in detail by one early Western writer:

Fifty miles east of Lo Yang, the confused loess hills which stretch eastward along the south bank of the Yellow river from the Shensi border end abruptly at the stream of [Ssu-shui]. The stream flows in a flat valley about a mile broad, bordered to the west by the loess hills which end in a steep slope. To the east the stream has in past ages scoured out a low, vertical cliff, on top of which the great plain begins; flat, featureless, dotted at intervals with villages in groves of trees. The stream itself, receding from the cliff in a course of time, now flows in the center of the sunken valley, with a stretch of flat land on either bank. The road from the east to Lo Yang and Shensi descends into the ravine, crossing the stream at the little city of Ssu-shui, before entering the hills by a narrow defile among precipices.

Li stayed in his powerful position on top of the cliffs on the west side of the pass. He was in no hurry. He held a strong defensive position, and every day saw his remaining force exhausting the supply of his opponent, bring closer the successful end of the siege in Luoyang. Li's strategy was reminiscent of Sunzi's maxim to first occupy a position of strength and then seek victory. Dou's wife suggested the he bypass Li's position altogether. They should move to the north and east of Li's position and attack his homeland in Taiyuan Province. This would unsettle Li's tactical position and weaken his claim to the mandate. If Dou was lucky, he could force Li to chase him. But Dou's generals overruled the plan. They were possibly bribed by Wang to make sure they relieved the siege at Luoyang, but they were definitely dismissive of a woman's opinion and considered her unworthy of giving them advice. On top of this, Dou's force might have had significant trouble leaving its logistical tether along the Yellow River.

After a month, Li finally advanced on Dou. The sources don't list an exact reason, but it's likely he believed the morale of his opponent's army had deteriorated, but he also didn't want Dou's men to retreat to the safety of their core territories. To entice them to battle, he sent a cavalry raid on Dou's supply lines and made his camp at the west side of the pass look like it was weakly held. Dou then deployed his troops into battle positions in the eastern side of the valley. Yet Li still waited. His opponent was arrayed in battle formation and didn't want to break ranks. This meant they were deployed all morning without eating, and they were starting to get stiff, hungry, and tired. By noon, Li finally sent a probing attack. When Dou's men withdrew in fear instead of attacking the probing force, Li launched an all-out assault.

Li charged into the thick of the fighting with his elite cavalry. One of his close relatives cut and hacked his way back and forth across the battlefield so many times that it was said his armor was filled with arrows like a porcupine. The key moment came when Li reached the east side of the valley and unfurled the Tang banner. Combined with a sudden flanking attack from the returning cavalry raid, Dou's forces scattered in fear. Over fifty thousand were taken prisoner, and Dou was killed trying to cross the river. The combined effect of capturing Luoyang a short time later in the west and the submission of most of Dou's forces and leaders in the east greatly helped Li consolidate his rule. Dou had controlled one of the key population and farming centers in the empire. With Dou Jiang defeated, Li had subdued his major rivals to his east and west, leaving only general mopping-up operations against holdouts.

TANG DYNASTY

During the period of disunion, Sui Wendi (541–604), who descended from mixed steppe-Chinese ancestors, founded the Sui dynasty in 581. Like the reign of the Qin dynasty, his was short, forfeited upon his death to the tyrannical emperor Yang-ti, which was quickly followed by the Tang dynasty in 618. The Tang formed one of the most vigorous and splendid periods in Chinese history.

The Tang dynasty benefitted from several policies started during the Sui dynasty. The empire recruited scholars and civil servants from prominent local families in various regions but also established the exam system, which increased the caliber of the civil servants. The exam system tested a potential civil servant's knowledge of the Confucian classics such as the *Analects* and also what eventually became the Seven Military Classics. Many

Opposite: The Tang dynasty, c. 750. The city of Taiyun was the provincial capital and power base from which the Tang dynasty sprung. They eventually captured and ruled from Luoyang and defeated their most significant rival at Hulao Pass. The map extends west to show Tang influence in the Tarim basin and oasis cities along the Silk Road, and the battle with Muslim forces at Talas.

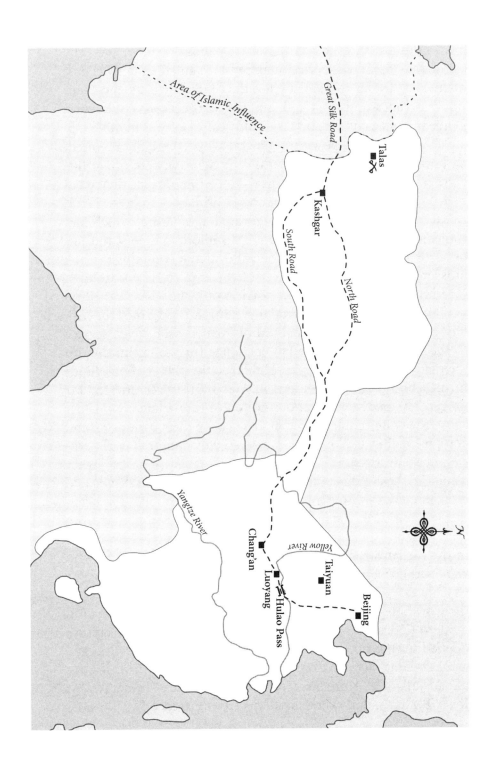

local families believed that having a family member pass the exam and enter civil service qualified it as an elite family. Thus, many local leaders became tied to the central dynasty and spent small fortunes on tutors and supplies so their sons could pass. Leaders from Chinese society could still rise from humble origins. An Lushan, a powerful general who eventually revolted, and other powerful figures within the dynasty were often illiterate foreigners with little cultural education. But the divide between the civil and military spheres continued.

The equal-field system reinvigorated agriculture, which had stagnated during the long period of disunion. In theory, the emperor owned all the land and then allocated it equitably (for the most part) among every subject of the empire. The state then taxed the land and received a portion of its goods or called on the farmers for physical labor. Part of this labor formed the *fubing* system. The *fubing* consisted of farmers who owed service to the state in times of war in exchange for tax exemption on their land. This was somewhat similar to the military households formed by other empires but was far more successful for far longer. The tax exemption did not constitute a huge bonus because the state required soldiers to supply their own arms and equipment. But it did create a cost effective and relatively efficient system for supplying soldiers. This concept is somewhat similar to the citizen-soldier ideal found in Republican Rome and the United States. In contrast to those ideals, though, these soldiers were tied to the land, the military obligation passed from father to son, and during the decline of the Tang dynasty, just as in the earlier Sui dynasty, the government regarded those who were part of *fubing* as little better than slaves, socially and legally.

Culturally, the Tang capital at Chang'an became the envy of the world. In size, significance, and diversity it had no rival until modern times. The population flourished, and Chinese culture opened itself to foreigners. The city lured traders, diplomats, gawkers, and people from every corner of the world. It contained Japanese, Koreans, Central Asians, Vietnamese, Arabs, Jews, Persians, and even Christians from Europe. The Tang repaired the Grand Canal that connected the Yellow and Yangtze Rivers. This allowed the opulent capital and densely populated regions of the north to import food and goods more easily from the south. It also contributed to cross-regional trade, and the resulting taxes added to the splendor of the dynasty.

As an emperor with a Chinese and nomadic background, Li Shimin, who was called Emperor Taizong (599–649), extended Chinese power into the steppes. His mixed ancestry provided him with a strong military background, and his close connections to steppe groups provided him with powerful cavalry. The unique combination of skills led to what historians call Li's "strategic trademark."[2] He would advance against an enemy and draw it into the field. He would make sure to have a stronger, fortified position than his enemy and better supplies. (In most cases this was fairly easy, considering that he was often outnumbered and smaller armies require less food.) When the enemy tired, he would dangle some kind of bait. He would either destroy his fortifications, or retreat a bit, or he would feign weakness or a lightly held position. When the enemy took the bait and attacked, he would use his cavalry as the tip of the spear to break his enemy's center and cause its psychological collapse. With the same cavalry, he would pursue the enemy relentlessly until he annihilated his opponents. The speed and maneuverability of his cavalry forces were particularly suited to this aggressive manner of combat. It was no surprise, then, that he expanded Chinese control far into the steppe and oasis cities along the Silk Road. The better military control over the Silk Road facilitated a transfer of knowledge and wealth across much of the Asian continent. He expanded Chinese control so far into central Asia that later Tang forces encountered Middle Eastern-based Muslim armies at the Battle of Talas River (751). They fought the Muslim armies near modern-day Afghanistan. Both sides were at the limits of their power, and the Tang dynasty was soon consumed with the An Lushan rebellion, but this was an important example of the scope and reach of the Tang dynasty.

In fact, the cultural achievements of this period set the standard for beauty and glory in Chinese history. Tang cultural accomplishment was cosmopolitan in nature. Music from central Asia entered along the trade routes. Merchants from Arabia and India set up quarters in southeastern China and brought their cultural tastes with them. Pottery figurines placed in Chinese tombs included traders and ladies from foreign courts. Nestorian Christians established churches, and their monuments provide important insight into the history of non-Western Christians. Poetry included romantic descriptions of foreign culture and places, such as exotic goods in the market or the far reaches of the Tang dynasty. An anthology of poetry from Li Bo (701–762) compiled during the Ming dynasty contained almost fifty thousand poems and stunningly beautiful imagery. Li Bo wrote about service on the frontier:

A Tartar horn tugs at the north wind,
Thistle Gate shines whiter than the stream.
The sky swallows the road to Kokonor.
On the Great Wall, a thousand miles of moonlight.

This period was also the golden age of Buddhism in China. Buddhism was first introduced during the period of disunion; the humble monasteries patronized by the emperors became centers of vast land and wealth during this dynasty. Not only were the monasteries rich, but the sophisticated beauty of their temples inspired awe. Few Buddhist temples have survived in China, but the architecture, wooden sculptures, and painted walls at the Hoyuji temple in Japan draw millions of tourists today. The monasteries sent monks across South Asia to learn from Indian scholars, and they often congregated in the capital. One recently excavated cave contained exquisite stone sculptures and thousands of ancient manuscripts. Buddhist temples often served as centers of learning and inns for their traveling colleagues or merchants. Scholarship continued as literacy spread. This included more dynastic histories, dictionaries, and also commentaries on the Confucian classics.

CHANGING CLASSIC TEXTS

The last of the Seven Military Classics, *Questions and Replies between Tang Taizong and Lei Weigong*, was written during this period. It is important to consider that the first of the military classics was likely completed a thousand years earlier, from the perspective of a small state seeking a powerful revolution against the dominant power. The last classic is a reported conversation between the current emperor and a military theorist. Society had changed, and the writers at this point were answering questions from a position of power instead of seeking power or vying for power among warring states. Some Chinese scholars claim there was little worthy or novel military theory beyond the end of the Warring States period. They claim they are useless theorizing from Confucian bureaucrats. But there is no specific evidence that early writers were military men. Many of them seemed more like a skilled class of advisers. And later writers did have a fair amount of military experience. On top of that, this is a collection of writings that summarizes statements from one of China's greatest military leaders (Li Shimin or Taizong). The writings also comment on specific battles and analyze them in light of classic military theory.[3]

It may seem like these disparate books, written by vastly different people in different positions at different times, don't fit together, but they were compiled in the later Song dynasty as a specific core of military readings designed to help aspiring commanders. Instead of looking at the differences, one might consider how each book treats warfare from a different position of power and with different goals and means. With a wide and substantive discussion of various concepts, from revolutionary warfare to preserving state power to the use of chariots changing to cavalry, it provides a future commander a broad foundation of knowledge. Reading these, an aspiring Chinese leader would know how to fight in a swamp or on the steppes; how to conduct river combat to topple an emperor; or how to defend a fortress using fire tactics.

In short, these classics provide a corpus of wisdom that could justify certain approaches, positions, and strategies. But because

they tended to be vague and often had contradictory information, they could actually support both sides of a position at the
same time. That tended to undermine their use as an ironclad
guide. Yet there is still plenty of evidence that the ruses and
strategies mentioned in them were used in battle. Every chapter
in this book you are reading thus far (and more to come) illustrates examples of strategies from these classics. Although it's
possible they were included by Confucian scholars writing their
history with knowledge of the classics, and not as a product of
thought that said, "I should follow this principle of [Han dynasty historian] Ssu Ma." In short, one might answer the question of their effectiveness like the medieval scholar Peter
Abelard's discussion of seemingly contradictory biblical principles, with a yes and no (*Sic et Non*).

WHY NOT CHINESE SAMURAI OR KNIGHTS?
This is a good place to consider the role of military technology
and why armies in China looked different than those in medieval
Europe, and why they even looked different than those in their
neighbor Japan. The answer lies in the relationships between geography, power, and population.

Chinese leaders never faced a situation such as those faced
by the Angevin English kings. These kings traced their ancestry
back to the Duke of Normandy and his 1066 invasion of England. Each in turn was the English king and also Duke of Normandy, and after Henry II married Eleanor of Aquitaine, he also
became Count of Anjou and Aquitaine. Thus he was a king but
actually held more territory as a vassal in France than as king
of England. This made his relationship with the French king particularly awkward and complicated during times of war. The
clear-cut delineation of power took hundreds of years to navigate. This kind of diffusion of power was quite common in Europe.[4]

The Chinese faced a bit of this during the period of disunion.
For example, Fu Jian's empire collapsed after Fei River at least
in part because he had too many fortress chiefs only nominally
loyal to him. And during periods of weakness, various govern-

ment officials rebelled and became independent chiefs. Unlike in Europe, this trend was an aberration and not the norm. A new emperor in China did negotiate power, but the cultural norms and power of the empire eventually absorbed the former rivals. Much like the Duke of Normandy, the governor of Taiyuan Province founded his own nation. But unlike Europe, once the Tangs gained power, they maintained strong control over the use of that power and their subordinate political leaders.

In Europe, this diffusion of power created a feudal system centered on a negotiated arrangement of delegating central power in exchange for the supply of knights. The Chinese also developed a form of warfare based on heavy cavalry and had a period of disunion with diffuse political power. But the Chinese polities consolidated politically under the Sui and Tang dynasties. The strong central government could raise large horse armies without a need to outsource it to its vassals. The control over the use of military power and the means of raising armies made China's medieval history far different than Europe's and meant the rise of a noble class of knights providing service as vassals to their king never occurred. The legalistic emperor commanded far more power than his medieval European counterparts.

The Chinese empires' use of large infantry-based armies with cavalry components rather than specialized warriors such as the samurai in Japan, followed a similar logic. Crossbows require less training than longbows, are easier to aim, and have more penetrating power (which is why they were banned by the pope in Europe). They can even be preloaded for immediate release upon sight of an enemy. The smaller missiles were easier to manufacture and transport. But they had a slower rate of fire (by almost six times) and shorter range than regular arrows. They can't be loaded and shot by somebody on horseback. All of this means they are ideally suited for use in large numbers, behind cover, and especially in the defense of a city.

The crossbow made large armies relatively easier to train, less expensive to equip, and far more deadly than their competitors. They were not especially well-suited to fighting in cavalry warfare, but they were well-suited to territories with large populations. As far back as the Warring States period, Chinese rulers could raise armies and train them to use the crossbow quickly compared to armies that relied on highly skilled individual warriors; as a result, they could confront an enemy in relatively short order. The dense population centers, technology that worked best in large formations, and weapons that could be used by raw conscripts, facilitated the use of substantial infantry armies. Combined with political considerations whereby power was not subcontracted to feudal vassals, this moved China away from the use of knights.[5]

In contrast, the samurai were highly skilled and trained. The population of Japan was often far smaller than that of China. The Japanese centers of power had less available farmland, which restricted the population growth, the number of potential recruits, and the size of an army. The armor and sword of a samurai could consume anywhere from six to nine months of a smith's time, and many months of income for the average peasant. Finally, the complex tactics needed to survive a fight with other samurai (which, contrary to popular knowledge, most often consisted of rival horse archers maneuvering around each other for a better shot) required years of intensive training.

One story is fairly typical of the exquisite training of the samurai. A father and son on a small rural estate awoke to thieves stealing a horse. Without any conversation, both warriors mounted their horses and sped off in pursuit. They often operated outside of each other's sight but coordinated their efforts to such a degree that it seemed planned. When they finally cornered one of the thieves, still out of sight of each other, the father yelled, "Shoot," and the thump of his son's bow was heard before the father's word faded away. The father called for his son to get the horse and rode home without a second thought. The son recovered the horse, and as he rode home, he was joined in twos and threes by his servants and retainers. By the time he reached home, he had a posse of thirty men in arms. He dismissed them and went to bed without checking in with his father. Their training was such that the father and son didn't need to check on each other, coordinate strategy, or even practice, but in the middle of the night and within hours, they had completed their mission.[6]

The average farmer didn't have the luxury of years of study. He labored most of the year on his farm to feed himself. The combination of technology and skill required made samurai skills a province of the elite. This meant that a handful of samurai were often the most that a lord or local elite could produce. Armies were composed of dozens of loosely connected groups of allies, retainers, relatives, and supporters. This made them incredibly unstable, and alliances based on coalitions of samurai were short lived and hard to maneuver on the battlefield. Power in Japan, then, was relatively more diffuse for much of its history. The combination of political power, geography, and technology made warfare in Japan (and to a certain extent Europe) the domain of relatively few numbers of samurai (and knights). In contrast, the relatively large population and ease of arming and training numbers of crossbow soldiers in China made infantry a much bigger component of its armies and meant there was no specialized class of warrior similar to the samurai.

CONCLUSION

Li Shimin's victories inaugurated one of the golden ages in Chinese history. They projected power farther than any dynasty previously had and exported Chinese culture throughout much of Asia. Military writers completed the Seven Military Classics in this period, and they were compiled by Confucians in the next dynasty. This period also showed the effects of military technology in China and how the emperors retained control over the use of force, with a resulting lack of focus on specialized cavalry components similar to knights and samurai. But China had yet to encounter a nomadic foe like the Mongols, who could adapt to different terrains and modes of combat.

# THE SIEGE OF XIANGYANG

## 1267–1273

[The Mongols] are most efficient in wars, having been in conflict with other nations for the space of these forty-two years. When they come to any rivers, the chief men of the company have a round and light piece of leather. They put a rope through the many loops on the edge of this, draw it together like a purse, and so bring it into the round form of a ball, which leather they fill with their garments and other necessaries, trussing it up most strongly. But upon the midst of the upper part thereof, they lay their saddles and other hard things; there also do the men themselves sit. This, their boat, they tie to a horse's tail, causing a man to swim before, to guide over the horse, or sometimes they have two oars to row themselves over. The first horse, therefore, being driven into the water, all the others' horses of the company follow him, and so they pass through the river. But the common soldiers have each his leather bag or satchel well sewn together, wherein he packs up all his trinkets, and strongly trussing it up hangs it at his horse's tail, and so he crosses the river.

—Friar Jon of Plano Carpini, 1245

My hair bristles through my helmet, the rain stops as I lean against the rail;
I look up at the sky and scream a bellowing war cry.

Over thirty years of accomplishments are now dust upon the
ground.
Eight thousand li of paths under rising cloud and moon I did
not rest
My hair turning white on a young man's head from despair
The humiliation of the Jingkang period is not removed
The indignation I feel as a subject
What time will it be extinguished
Let me drive off in a chariot to trample and break
Their base at Helan Mountain.
My greater goal is to dine on the flesh of barbarians,
Laughing and discussing, I will quench my thirst with their
blood
Then, I will rest and wait to restore
Slake my thirst with the blood of the tribesmen.
I will rest and start afresh to recover the former lands of the
empire,
Then report to the emperor.
                    —attributed to Yue Fei, *The Whole River Red*

S IX YEARS. That's how long the commander Lu Wenhuan held
 out against the Mongols. But that was all up in smoke across
the Han River from him. He commanded the twin cities of Xiangyang and Fangcheng against the Mongol threat, and from
his vantage in Xiangyang, he witnessed the fall of Fangcheng.
Between their rise in the early thirteenth century in central Asia
and the beginning of the campaign against the Song in 1259,
the Mongols had ranged from Europe as far west as the Adriatic
Sea (on the east coast of Italy) to across both the Near and Middle East. But the wealth of southern China beckoned them, and
the sometimes-inept performance of the Chinese armies only encouraged them. Yet the southern Song dynasty effectively relied
upon the rivers and rough terrain of southern China to thwart
their attacks.

As was usual in Chinese history, southern China had the advantages of natural obstacles. The Mongol advance bogged
down in the Sichuan Basin, and faced a series of Chinese defensive works that were quite impressive: they were usually built

on cliffs near pivotal river crossings, both of which made cavalry charges and storming them difficult. The fortresses enclosed land within their walls where the besieged could farm. Each fort often had its own well for water, which enhanced the residents' ability to survive long sieges. And being on the rivers allowed the Song navy to resupply the forts fairly easily. This made the Mongols shift focus from the Sichuan valley to the pivotal cities of Xiangyang and Fangcheng along the Han River.[1]

Xiangyang and its twin city Fangcheng across the river were vital for control of the Middle Yangtze region, and the region was the launching point of Song counterattacks. But the Song court had political problems that helped the Mongols. The founders of the Song dynasty had intermarried with the military families based in the north. On top of that, many civilian officials held military commands, which further strengthened the ties between the court and the military. But when they moved to the south, they lost those advantages. The northern families were no longer closely related to members of the imperial family. The civilian officials became disconnected from policy, and regional concerns often trumped national policies. But this still wasn't a catastrophic situation throughout the mid-thirteenth century. The Lu clan, headed by Lu Wende, had significant ties with the court and family members in very important commands, such as his son, Lu Wenhuan, and his cousin, who commanded the important twin cities.

The Lu clan held these pivotal cities against the Mongols. Over a century earlier, one of the most acclaimed generals in all Chinese history, Yue Fei, launched attacks on the Mongols from this region. It protected a pivotal tributary to the Yangtze River and the centers of strength of the Song court. The navies that assisted Yang Su and his conquest on behalf of the Sui dynasty launched from this city, for example. Unfortunately, Lu Wende died during the early days of the siege. He had been one of the few generals to defeat the Mongols, and he cultivated good relations in the capital through a network of relatives and friends. His death inspired the chief minister to appoint a new overall commander of the defense, and the decision was based more on the new individual's political connections than the military needs. The court was nervous about the Lu clan and didn't want to grant the generals too much power.

The alienation and then defection of key generals due to disagreements with the court was a real concern. Another general, Lui Zheng, was the subject of baseless accusations of misusing funds, and he defected to the Mongols a few years before the siege began. He likely did so based on examples such as Yue Fei. Despite a stellar military career that is one of the most storied in Chinese history, Yue was imprisoned over being a too-vocal advocate of reclaiming the north and opposing a peace treaty with the Mongols. The court forced him to commit suicide a short time later. Lui Zheng knew that the court was paralyzed by factional infighting and couldn't be trusted. It couldn't properly direct strategy and continued to strain relations with many of its generals. The Mongols, in contrast, had the strategic initiative, could choose the time and place of their battle, and treated defecting generals rather well. The first two circumstances allowed the Mongols to have local superiority of forces and capture a key line of southern Song defense. The third matter came to the forefront quickly when the Mongols suggested that Le Wenhuan should also defect because of the court's distrust.

Lu Wende knew the Mongols were preparing a long siege, but his planned spoiling attack north and east of the twin cities evaporated upon his death. The western city of Xiangyang was protected by mountains on three sides and the Han River on its east. The city of Fangcheng had the river to its west, and was relatively exposed on its east side, so the siege started there. The first thing the Mongols did was start to break the link between the cities and fight off the Song navy, which was their chief avenue of supply. Through a series of bitter battles and fire attacks, the Mongols burned most of the Song ships and the bridge between the cities. Under a hail of Song arrows from Fangcheng, the Mongols erected their Muslim-engineered trebuchets. The Chinese developed special nets that largely negated the effect of the trebuchets, but the Mongol stranglehold on Fangcheng continued.

This is where the death of Lu Wende affected the defense. The new overall commander was a political hack who was largely unable to coordinate a defense of Fangcheng and managed only a few partial resupplies, with thousands dying upon each attempt. Worst of all, his appointment, which bypassed the capable defenders already fighting in the twin cities from the Lu clan, signaled to the Lu that they had lost the confidence of the court.

In early 1273, six years into the siege, the Mongols upgraded their trebuchets, and the Song forces had run low on food supplies. Under the cover of the thunderous impacts of massive hurled stones and raging snowstorms, the Mongols assaulted Fangcheng from every side (including an amphibious assault from the river to its west). The Mongol attackers suffered horrendous casualties, and many commanders from both sides were severely wounded as the soldiers filled trenches, stormed the walls, burned the city, and took part in desperate hand-to-hand fighting in the streets.

The Mongols killed everybody in Fangcheng and stacked their bodies. The ten thousand men, women, and children rose higher than the walls of the city and could be seen from Xiangyang. Lu Wenhuan assessed the situation. Western readers might assume that Lu Wenhuan would never join his enemy after a bitter fight that lasted most of the decade (and killed his family members). But generals had an obligation to save the men under their command from useless slaughter, and philosophically he could justify his defection if he believed that his rulers had lost the mandate. The Mongols' removal of the defector and Lu's chief rival, Lui Zheng, from the battlefield was a key sign of respect, which showed Lu he might defect successfully. Lu had fought for over six years with no resupply coming, and the knowledge that his city could fall like its sister across the river and its inhabitants would receive the same fate, combined with his continued alienation from the court, made him ready to concede.

The Jin and Southern Song dynasties, c. 1270. Both the Jin (in 1234) and Southern Song (in 1279) fell to the Mongols. The Mongol effort to conquer southern China started at Tongchuan and Chengdu, near the head waters of the Yangtze, but then shifted to the twin cities of Xiangyang and Fangcheng, which opened up the way to the Song capital at Jianking.

The Han River and a path to the Yangtze and the heart of the Song dynasty were now open to the invaders. The Mongols were an impressive military machine, but the Song dynasty had the resources and talented leaders to beat them. In many ways it was the political decisions of the southern Song court—such as its failure to adopt a proactive strategy, the alienation of key generals such as the Lu clan, and political appointments and divided command—that undermined the twin cities.

This chapter looks at the cultural developments that arose during the Song and Yuan dynasties, the interplay between the martial and cultural values *wu* and *wen*, and how the traditional interpretation of the Song dynasty collapsing because of its military weakness is not entirely accurate. And it will reveal that individual poor decisions of Song political leaders often hampered the actions of generals, caused some leaders to defect, hurt the dynasty's strategic outlook, and often failed to control the potent and aggressive new ideology called neo-Confucianism.

SONG DYNASTY

A general powerful and talented enough to protect the frontier also held enough power to assert his will against the central government. Strong emperors held these individuals in check, but a strong general named An Lushan rebelled in 755. The long period of peace and prosperity of the Tang dynasty resulted in militarization along the frontiers with relatively few units and seasoned soldiers stationed near the capital along the Yellow River. The soldiers stationed near the capital were often vanity assignments given to noble families. The checks and balances that the government held against frontier generals using their force without government permission weakened through the first couple of centuries during the dynasty. When the inevitable revolt of a powerful general happened, it meant there were only a few untrained armies to oppose him. This rebellion shattered the strength of the dynasty and led to another period of regional warlords, with the last weak emperor deposed in 907. The central government had to cede power to local governors in exchange for military support. Eventually the local rulers abandoned the pretext of continued central rule by the Tang dynasty.

After a brief period of disunion, one of these leaders, Taizu (924–976), established the Song dynasty in 960. Finding a monetary economy more efficient than bartering, the government increasingly paid farmers in metal coins. Since the cash rates for their goods stayed consistent, the farmers sold their surplus on the market. New strains of rice increased the productivity and yield of the average acre, which in turn increased population and wealth. While the Tang had enjoyed restaurants, theaters, wine shops, brothels, and acrobats, those establishments and individuals now catered to the increasing number of new rich and local officials (also paid in coin). While the population of the largest city of Europe during this time was roughly sixty thousand people, that of the Song capital at Kaifeng was almost one million people. The trend of increasing southern power and population continued, as the southern capital of Hangzhou had a population nearing two million. Merchants based in southern ports, with the help of their new invention, the compass, and new ship designs traveled far around the world, from Japan in the north to Sumatra in the south, where middlemen then took their goods as far as the Horn of Africa.

The north remained vital as well. Chinese workers invented new coal- and iron-smelting techniques that provided them with carbonized steel, the material that led to some of the best weapons in the world. Block-print presses churned out books to the point that they were fairly common. Presses began printing Buddhist texts as early as the seventh century, and by the mid-Song, books with moveable type were more common. Military leaders incorporated gunpowder weapons into their armies such as primitive guns called fire cannons and early forms of grenades.[2]

Many of the Chinese cultural achievements in this period centered on the gentry scholar. The exam system continued to cull the best and brightest from leading Chinese families into civil service and also acted as a stamp of approval on a family's status. So many people from the south qualified for government service that the emperor had to set regional quotas. Song pottery became widespread, and every major area and city had a kiln. Artists created new refining techniques, a variety of glazes, and under the influence of Confucianism and Daoism, their shapes were restrained and harmonious.

Historians continued to write comprehensive works. Sima Guang (1019–1086) wrote *A Comprehensive Mirror for Aid in Government*, which surveyed the entire expanse of Chinese history. As mentioned before, Song officials compiled the salient works of Chinese military theory into the Seven Military Classics of ancient China to aid in the training of their officers. Poets during this period increasingly considered the lives of nontraditional women but still wrote in awe of those from the Tang dynasty.

NEO-CONFUCIANISM

Neo-Confucianism started as a renaissance of traditional Confucian values and as a reaction to the influence of Buddhism and religious Daoism. The first true pioneer was the writer Zhou Dunyi (1017–1073) who argued, unlike Buddhists, that reality existed and could be understood. Zhu Xi (1130–1200) was an influential Chinese philosopher, whose role in Chinese history can be compared to that of Thomas Aquinas (1224–1274) in Europe. Zhu Xi combined the metaphysical ideas that had permeated Chinese society with Confucian teachings. With his emphasis on meditation, some contemporary critics argued that he was only a Buddhist wolf in neo-Confucian sheep's clothing. His supporters responded that he emphasized "quiet sitting" as a way to fundamentally inculcate Confucian ideals and wisdom. Historians also point out that his teachings became one more source of stability in China as it endured conquest dynasties, dynasties established by outside conquerors. In short, in contrast to Buddhists and Daoists, neo-Confucians did not believe in some kind of spiritual world that was disconnected from the physical. Overall, they took a more rationalist approach and rejected what they saw as the more superstitious elements of Daoism and Buddhism.

Politically, neo-Confucians tended to be rather aggressive. They often called for the reconquest of lost territories. They were morally and religiously intolerant of the kind of political and military compromises the court needed to make. Because of their moral connections to classic Confucianism and influence with the court, they were a potent force to deal with. For example, while the desire for reconquest might seem compatible with the wishes of military leaders, it wasn't always so. The neo-Confucians were zealously intent on maintaining civilian control over the military. They scoffed at the recommendations of military men; even the more cultured and well connected ones who approached them had to do so with finesse. Gains in territory meant generals became more powerful. As their power grew, they became a threat to the court and aroused suspicion among men who thought the military should remain subservient to civilians. The aggressive neo-Confucianists had a variety of tools to limit military control, such as marginalizing the officers they didn't like through false accusations, cutting off their contact to the emperor, overbearing administrative action, playing favorites, and even executing some. This often forced the emperor to walk a delicate line between pleasing religious zealots at home and irredentist generals on the frontier, trying to maintain good relationships with and between the two groups, and not abdicating too much power to either group. With that kind of juggling act, it's a small wonder the Southern Song Empire lasted as long as it did and stands as a testament to the strength of Chinese armies and their skilled leadership.

### MILITARY WEAKNESS AND THE MONGOL RULE

A conquest dynasty is a dynasty founded through military force by, in the case of China, non-Chinese people. The Chinese usually faced a problem with their nomadic neighbors to the north and west. The Qin built the first segments of what is now the Great Wall in the second century BC to try to repel them. The Han dynasty alternated between expensive campaigns to subdue them and giving them expensive gifts of silk and princesses. The Xiongnu, an early nomadic tribe, helped speed the collapse of the dynasty after the War of the Eight Princes. The period of disunion was replete with nomadic armies, and even the founder of the Tang dynasty, Li Shimin, excelled in the use of nomadic-style heavy cavalry as his tactical finishing force. Nomadic horsemen aided An Lushan in his great rebellion. And every emperor tried to have contingents of cavalry supplied by friendly tribal leaders. Hence, it was not unusual to see nomads attack China and even have success. What was unusual was the amount of territory the Mongols conquered, the longevity of their presence, their ability to operate in a variety of terrains, and the astoundingly foolish choices of the Song dynasty that resulted in its demise.

The Song reacted to the Mongols in the early thirteenth century the way Chinese did with other nomadic powers from the past. Strong leaders fought the nomads or tried to support rival claimants to the throne in attempts to have them fight each other. Weaker rulers offered them goods and princesses, essentially buying them off. Incompetent leaders did neither effectively. The southern Song fit this last category. By the end of the twelfth century, the Song had lost a great deal of territory to the nomadic tribe called the Jurchens. Chinese leaders believed that the enemy of their enemy was their friend and sided with the Mongols against the Jurchens in an attempt to reclaim their lost territory. After the defeat of their mutual enemy, the Song betrayed the Mongols and recaptured some of their northern territory assigned to the Mongols.[3]

In attacking the Song, the Mongols changed tactics and relied on Chinese defections to reorganize their forces and adjust their strategy in southern China. This revealed a trend in Chinese history. Since the founding of the Qin dynasty, civil servants often had more loyalty to the concept of China than to a particular dynasty. Thus, when a dynasty seemed in disarray, as though it had lost the Mandate of Heaven, civil servants felt no particular duty to go down with the ship. Instead, they served the group that was winning and proving its claim to the mandate. Chinese scholars and elites maintained their status and positions. The Mongol ruler Kublai Kahn (1215–1294) sought the riches of China and thought that the civil servants were the most likely to help him administer the already conquered northern territories and conquer the rest. Kublai Kahn also found that the rituals of leadership, such as wearing silk robes and performing religious ceremonies, earned him legitimacy in the eyes of those he sought to conquer. So the Mongol leaders, civil servants, and defecting generals found a mutually beneficial agreement that sapped the strength of the Song dynasty.

## A CIVIL CULTURE THAT CAN'T FIGHT?

The fall of the Song dynasty also highlighted a much broader trend in Chinese history: the general perception of military weakness. The dynasty collapsed in the face of outside pressure, though it arguably defended itself against the Mongol threat longer than any other nation had, and much longer than the quickly supine Europeans. Even then, Confucian historians argued that the Mongol adoption of Chinese rituals, customs, and style of rule proved that Chinese culture won. As discussed earlier, Confucian historians also emphasized a dichotomy between *wu* (martial) and *wen* (civil). The works of Confucius and many of the Buddhist writers contained strains of antimilitarism. Few generals were literate or capable of writing their own histories similar to Caesar's *Gallic Wars*; thus, official histories often neglected and sometimes denigrated military affairs. In addition to the bias of Chinese historians, early Western historians added to the neglect of Chinese military history. Jesuits first disseminated stories of Chinese customs, history, and culture to the West, but they often focused on molding Confucian rituals into proper Christian behavior. As a consequence, the first Western histories of China faced the double bias of Christian missionaries largely interested in religion and science reading histories from Confucian scholars who were at best apathetic to the military. This trend continued through the modern period and is even reflected in many textbooks today that point to the Song dynasty as the emblematic weak dynasty.

The fall of the northern Song was not a foregone conclusion. Even during this period of supposed cultural supremacy over the military, the empire still had military leaders who were well read and civilian bureaucrats who led armies with some success. They failed in some respects more because of so-called "peace disease" than any rejection of military culture. Peace disease is the shorthand phrase for a military that has been at peace for so long it has few soldiers with military experience and little institutional memory of the last war. As a result, it tends to fight poorly early in a war, but once it gains a skilled set of warriors and leaders, it performs far better. The Song wars with the neighboring Tangut nation in the eleventh century were fought generations apart from each other, but the supposedly inept northern Song eventually fought well enough to create a favorable peace with Tangut. The Song's poor performance was the result of troops and leaders who were simply untrained and unpracticed from years of peace and not because of some kind of long-term cultural aversion to or rejection of war.

The fall of Kaifeng and the end of the dynasty were due more to the stunningly inept political decisions of the emperor. During the pivotal military campaign, he scattered his armies across northern China and failed to realize the importance of the capital and his personal presence, which turned an admittedly devastating raid into the collapse of political power. The armies being dispersed allowed the Jurchens to capture Kaifeng and the emperor. This threw the entire government apparatus and defense of the north into disarray. Even after that, strong generals arose, the greatest of whom, Yue Fei, was successful on the battlefield. He started his military career as a small unit leader before the fall of Kaifeng. After its fall (the "humiliation" mentioned in the second epigraph at the beginning of this chapter), he reorganized Chinese defenses, and over the next thirty years (also mentioned in the epigraph), he won a string of victories that made him one of China's most legendary and skilled generals. Yet he was killed because of political fighting and factional machinations.

Even after all the decisions that robbed the empire of half its territory and some of its most skilled generals fighting against Jurchen raiders, the southern Song managed to battle the Mongols to a standstill for forty years, using key fortifications, the benefit of geography, and capable emperors. In contrast, many states across Asia and Europe collapsed after a single campaign, while the weakest dynasty in Chinese history had the latent strength to survive much longer. Similar trends can be seen in every other period of Chinese history. Contrary to being an example of China's cultural preference for civil matters and rejection of military ones, this period shows that China was far more balanced between the two principles.

CONCLUSION

The siege of Xiangyang was the key event that led to the destruction of the Song dynasty. The Chinese defenders had plenty of men and material to resist the Mongol invasion. Due to court politics and the disputes with neo-Confucian court officials, the court policy was often paralyzed and ineffective. Despite the catastrophic military defeats, China still produced many military men with cultural attainments, as well as Confucian officials who could lead armies. Of course, the desperately poor who started their careers as outlaws could command society as well, as will be seen in the next chapter with the founding of the Ming dynasty.

# THE BATTLE OF LAKE POYANG

## 1363

Upon arriving at foreign countries, capture those barbarian kings who resist civilization and are disrespectful, and exterminate those bandit soldiers that indulge in violence and plunder. The ocean routes will be safe thanks to this, and foreigners will rely on them to secure their livelihood

—Zheng He

When you have left the city of Soochow and have traveled for four days through a splendid country, passing a number of towns and villages, you arrive at the most noble city of Hangzhou, which is in our language "City of Heaven." I will enter into particulars about its magnificence since the city is beyond dispute the finest and noblest in the world.

First and foremost, then, Hangzhou is so great that it is 200 square miles. In it there are 12,000 bridges of stone, with most so lofty that a great fleet could pass beneath them. And let no man marvel that there are so many bridges, for you see the whole city stands as it were in the water and surrounded by water, so that a great many bridges are required to give free passage around it. . . . Inside the city there is a lake of some 30 miles: and all round it are beautiful palaces and mansions, of the richest and most exquisite structure that you can imagine, belonging to the nobles of the city. There are also two islands, on each of which stands a rich, beautiful, and spacious edifice, furnished in such style fit for the palace of an emperor. And when anyone of the citizens desire to hold a marriage feast or to give any other entertainment, it is done at one of these palaces. And everything would be found there ready to order, such as silver plate, trenchers, and dishes (napkins and table cloths), and whatever else was needed.

This city of Hangzhou is the seat of one of the kings who rules over 100 great and wealthy cities. For in the whole of this part of the country, there are more than 1,200 great cities, without counting the towns and villages, which are also in great numbers. In each of those 1,200 cities the Great Khan has a garrison, and the smallest of such garrisons musters 1,000 men; while there are some of 10,000, 20,000, and 30,000; so that the total number of troops is something scarcely calculable. You must not suppose they are by any means all cavalry; a very large proportion are foot-soldiers, according to the special requirements of each city. And all of them belong to the army of the Great Khan. . . . On the lake there are numbers of boats and barges of all sizes for parties of pleasure. These will hold 10, 15, 20, or more persons, and are from 15 to 20 paces in length, with flat bottoms and ample breadth of beam, so that they always keep afloat. Anyone who desires to go with the women or with a party hires one of these barges which are always to be found completely furnished with tables and chairs and all the other apparatus for a feast. The roof forms a level deck, on which the crew stands and poles the boat along whithersoever may be desired for the lake is not more than two paces in depth. The inside of this roof and the rest of the interior is covered with ornamental painting in gay colors, with windows all round that can be shut or opened, so that the party at table can enjoy all the beauty and variety of the prospects on both sides as they pass along. The lake is never without a number of other such boats, laden with pleasure parties, for it is the great delight of the citizens here, after they have finished the day's business, to pass the afternoon in enjoyment with their ladies, either in these barges or in driving about the city in carriages.

—Marco Polo

Z HU YUANZHANG would eventually become the founder of the Ming dynasty (1368–1644). By the time he reached Lake Poyang in 1363, he was desperate and close to collapse. The Mongol-led Yuan dynasty had faltered, which led to the rise of a number of independent warlords. Zhu rose from little more than pirate captain of a dozen people to a position as a key warlord on the Middle Yangtze based on a powerful but loosely loyal coalition around the cities of Nanchang and Nanjing. But he was squeezed between two other powers vying for control. Chen Youliang up the river had much larger forces and outnumbered Zhu almost ten to one. Down the river was Zhang Shicheng. Luckily for Zhu, his southern rival was indolent and spent most of his time consolidating his power around the river, or Zhu's regime would have been strangled in its crib.

Despite the reprieve, Zhu was hardly in a good position. The rivers, marshes, and lack of roads in the region concentrated power in a handful of cities. And the leaders, Zhu and his rivals Chen and Zhang, required outstanding victories to maintain the loyalty of their loose coalitions of followers. Only capturing a major city provided the kind of spectacular victory to keep the followers loyal. This meant almost nonstop warfare for control of a handful of major cities along the Yangtze.

Chen Youliang sailed downriver to capture Nanchang in 1363. The main part of his fleet was massive tower ships. Their three decks were protected by large, castle-like fortifications on each deck and could transport up to three thousand men each. Combined with numerous smaller vessels, his fleet transported over three hundred thousand men. He planned to sail right next to the city walls and directly assault them from his ships. Zhu had expected this, though, and built new city walls away from the river's edge. Frustrated but not deterred, Chen disembarked his soldiers and conducted a standard siege of the city. Disembarking his soldiers had already undermined the timing of his plan, and through eighty-five days of fierce fighting with extensive use of cannon and firearms, the city still hadn't fallen.

It was only at this point that Zhu entered Lake Poyang. His tardiness represented his weakened position, as he had to spend over three months subduing a rebellion on the other side of his territory. Zhu didn't have any tower ships, and his one thousand ships and one hundred thousand men were vastly outnumbered, outsized, and outgunned. His advantage was represented in his smaller ships with more maneuverability. The fall of Nanchang after previous losses combined with his precarious position would have been a devastating blow from which he likely couldn't recover. The desperate nature of his position led to his unusually aggressive behavior during the battle. Chen, in contrast, only had to outlast his enemy and secure the city that was ready to fall.

Zhu positioned his fleet at the northern entrance to the lake to prevent his opponent's escape. Chen left a small force around the Nanchang and set sail to meet him. The battle was joined in late August 1363 as Zhu's ships charged at the larger fleet opposing them. The tower ships were quite formidable and dealt heavy damage to the Zhu's Ming fleet despite its use of fire and gunpowder ships. The first day's battle ended in a draw, and the badly outnumbered Ming fleet suffered as much damage as it caused. The next day the Ming tried even more fire attacks. Ships filled with straw, gunpowder, and other flammable material were launched at the enemy, this time with dummy fire ships to aid the attack. Chen's forces were in a tight formation around the tower ships, acting as the backbone of the fleet. This increased their firepower against the smaller ships but made the fire attacks more successful. These attacks destroyed several hundred ships and killed about sixty thousand people. It is a testament to the strength of the Chen fleet that this was seen as just a setback instead of a crippling defeat. If Chen held a tight formation, then Zhu launched fire attacks. If Chen loosened his formation, the smaller Ming ships would close to try to grapple and board their enemies. But in any case, the damage Chen inflicted was usually accomplished only through heavy losses to his own fleet and wasn't enough for the decisive victory he needed.

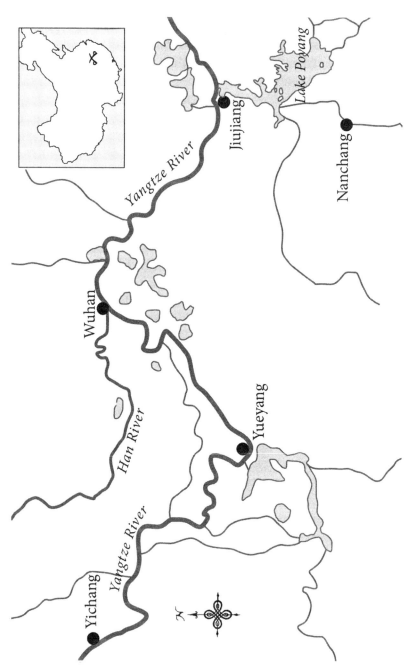

The Battle of Lake Poyang, 1363. The rough terrain of southern China made control of the few cities vital, from Yichang (at the end of the Three Gorges region) to Nanchang.

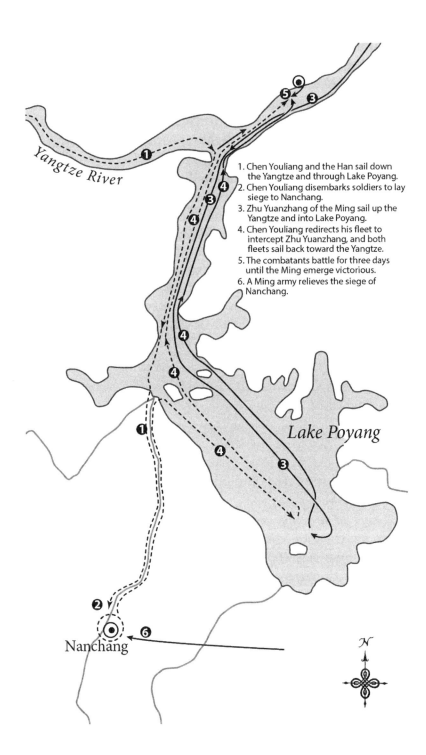

1. Chen Youliang and the Han sail down the Yangtze and through Lake Poyang.
2. Chen Youliang disembarks soldiers to lay siege to Nanchang.
3. Zhu Yuanzhang of the Ming sail up the Yangtze and into Lake Poyang.
4. Chen Youliang redirects his fleet to intercept Zhu Yuanzhang, and both fleets sail back toward the Yangtze.
5. The combatants battle for three days until the Ming emerge victorious.
6. A Ming army relieves the siege of Nanchang.

By this time, though, a separately dispatched land force had relieved the siege of Nanchang. That was good news for Zhu, but after several days of fierce fighting, fire attacks, and attempts of his ships to grapple and seize their enemies, the battle was largely a draw. Chen's larger force had been damaged, but its land forces could still capture the city after they drove away the smaller Ming fleet.

By September, the two sides had separated. Zhu moved back to the north end of the lake to prevent Chen's possible escape. Chen waited on the southern side of the lake. For almost a month, both sides eyed each other warily. Chen couldn't resume the siege of Nanchang with a large rival fleet ready to engage him at any time. And he didn't want to force his larger ships through a narrow channel, against the current, and with the Ming penchant for fire attacks. By the beginning of October, Chen's food supplies were running low, and he couldn't keep his army and fleet, which formed the center of his power, so far from his core territories. He charged the Ming position. The resulting battle descended into a chaotic melee of fights between individual ships floating downriver. It may have resulted in another draw or perhaps a victory for Chen, but reminiscent of the fate of Harold at the Battle of Hastings, a stray arrow hit and killed Chen Youliang. His son and heir and fifty thousand soldiers were captured, and hundreds of ships were destroyed.[1]

This was the spectacular victory that Zhu Yuanzhang needed. He still had to consolidate territory up and downstream from his core territories on the Yangtze and complete the destruction of the Yuan dynasty. But he had gone a long way to strengthening his position, expanding his core, and defeating a chief rival for power. The Ming dynasty Zhu founded would rule for hundreds of years and established important historical precedents. This victory at Lake Poyang also gives us a chance to examine the use of naval power throughout Chinese history and revisit the impact of technology by considering why gunpowder weapons weren't used as extensively and to the same cultural effect as in Europe.

## THE MING DYNASTY

After the death of Kublai Khan in 1294, the Mongol rulers quickly lost effectiveness. Like many rulers from the steppe, they were never Chinese enough in their customs and culture to earn the trust of the indigenous people. Often, to maintain power and preserve their ethnic heritage in a sea of Han Chinese, they segregated themselves from their conquered subjects. But they did become Chinese enough to clash with their relatives and tribe mates on the steppe. Those relatives often revolted against the Mongols, which in turn sapped their military strength. With the weakening of military power and central authority, China again devolved into a series of regional powers led by warlords.

One of these warlords, Zhu Yuanzhang, started his career essentially as a river pirate in the Middle Yangtze. By 1363, he had consolidated his power by winning one of the most climactic naval battles in Chinese history at Lake Poyang. By 1367, he had gained control over much of China and inaugurated the Ming dynasty. The first emperors continued to expand their realm. They humbled the Mongols through numerous campaigns into the steppes and reasserted their authority over regions as far south as Vietnam and as far north as Korea. They also gained control of many of the oasis cities on the eastern end of the Silk Road.

One of the most important aspects of the Ming dynasty was the trading missions it launched. As the Middle Kingdom, the Chinese wished to expand their tributary system. Just as internal Confucian ideals stressed the loyalty of a son to his father, and the father to the emperor, their international relations were often viewed as father/son, or elder/younger brother, with China as the dominant partner. The expeditions of Zheng He (1371–1435?), for example, contained sixty-two major ships and over twenty-eight thousand sailors. Zheng He's fleet traded as far away as east Africa and dominated local politics in many places they visited. They installed a new king in Java and captured hostile kings in places such as Borneo. They also brought back exotic gifts such as giraffes and zebras.

This happened almost half a century before the voyages of Columbus but raises the question, why was it Europeans and not the Chinese who established trading outposts across the world and discovered the Americas? Zheng's voyages, despite the impressiveness of their scope, stopped almost as soon as they began. Many of the early Confucian classics, such as those by Mencius, denigrated the pursuit of money, and many emperors had laws that restricted merchant activities. This stood in stark contrast to early Italian capitalists such as Marco Polo and Christopher Columbus and their sponsors, who acted somewhat similarly to modern venture capitalists. Chinese culture had stood at the center of the Middle Kingdom for almost two millennia. The Chinese had lent their script and culture to many neighbors, and they assimilated those who subjected them to military defeat, such as the nomadic invaders who continually pressed the court along China's northern border. They felt little desire to explore and set up far-flung trading posts. China also lacked the competition dynamic found in European society. Italian city states, the newly unified country of Spain, England, and France all competed for the same wealth and control of trade routes, and this spurred innovation and risk taking among Westerners that their Chinese counterparts often lacked.

As the Ming dynasty went on, it did start to increase its participation in national and world trade. Some historians estimate that half of the silver that came from the New World ended up in China. Just as new bronze coins helped stimulate trade and the prosperity of the average farmer during the Song dynasty, the introduction of silver coins did the same in the Ming dynasty. The average farmer had access to better seeds and fertilizer, and paid only a single tax. This increased prosperity also contributed to a greater increase in population. The large population allowed the government to take in surpluses, even as it kept taxes low, and maintain a fully manned and aggressive military. The people obtained this silver from local mines in the mountains of southern China but also from a new worldwide trading network. As the sixteenth century progressed, European traders established outposts around the world, and more gold and silver flowed from the Americas. (In fact, his haul along the America-to-China route helped propel Sir Francis Drake to pirate fame.)

Painting, poetry, music, literature, and theater flourished during the Ming dynasty. Artists in this period painted lacquer wares, applying a fine polish to porcelain items, which included rather detailed and intricate scenes. The wealthy usually bought these works, in addition to fine furniture and latticework, and arranged them according to aesthetic and Daoist tastes. The latter dictated that the arrangement of furniture must conform to the flow of the room and location of the building.

Writing became even more prolific in this period. Newspapers began to use moveable-type printing. This made them easier to produce and increased their durability. Travel literature recorded the thoughts and experiences of writers who visited various parts of China. Xu Xiake (1587–1641) wrote a four-hundred-thousand-character diary that included everything from local geography to mineralogy. Writers started to compose their works in vernacular Chinese. This expanded readership to women, merchants, and shop clerks who only had a rudimentary education.

The late Ming period witnessed the first arrival of Jesuit missionaries from Europe. In 1607, some of these missionaries worked with the Chinese mathematicians to translate the Greek mathematical works into Chinese. Chinese scholars were impressed with European knowledge in some subjects, such as astronomy and geography. Most Chinese, however, were suspicious and critical of Christianity. Yet despite this tension, the Imperial Astronomical Board employed Western missionaries learned in science.

NAVAL MATTERS

Many historians and students consider China to be a traditional land power. This perception is somewhat correct, as China did not have extensive blue-water navies—ocean-going vessels and capital ships designed to operate in blue, or deep, water—

throughout much of its history. As described above, it did have treasure fleets during the Ming dynasty and extensive overseas trade. So overall, the perception is correct, but it discounts the extensive internal history and use of navies.

Given the country's numerous rivers and extensive coastal regions, and the fierce combat in and around rivers using marines and naval forces, Chinese naval history needs to include these small, brown-water ships—vessels which operate in swamps, marshes, and littorals. This reinterpretation would mean that throughout its history, Chinese military operations are replete with naval maneuvers. There are many examples we have seen: the Han dynasty couldn't control some southern kingdoms that broke away from Qin, because they were small coastal provinces in southern China, difficult to reach by land and protected by a small but well-trained fleet; the Tang dynasty scored a huge naval victory over Japan in the sixth century, which allowed it to expand and resupply its armies in the area; the northern Song dynasty collapsed in the face of the steppe tribe onslaught in the twelfth century on the plains in and around Kaifeng, but the southern Song saved themselves for over thirty years because of their impressive navy. The Song had lost most of their northern territory and faced a massive invasion from the Jurchens, but the southern Song navy broke the pontoon bridge of the invading force, severing the invading armies' logistical connection, and prevented them from retreating to the north side of the river. The eight-thousand-man naval force of the southern Song dynasty tied down a one-hundred-thousand-man army for a significant amount of time. A short time later, it faced another engagement, and despite being outnumbered six to one, the Song navy charged into the much larger force, secure in its superior training, and annihilated the opposing fleet. The Mongols understood the power of a navy and reportedly built five thousand warships and mustered seventy thousand marines to help conquer the southern Song stronghold of Xiangyang. A century later, Zhu Yuanzhang founded the Ming dynasty through the strength of his naval fleet. In fact, the brown-water navy he defeated had ships large enough to carry three thousand people. Throughout Chinese history, would-be invaders stretching back to the time of Cao Cao often had massive fleets and ships large enough to fire siege equipment.

But naval power wasn't only useful for securing power, it helped in keeping power. The last Song emperor was captured in a naval battle near Hong Kong. Likewise, the remnants of the Ming dynasty were defended by their fleet on a small island in southern China. The Qing would realize the need for a strong navy when British ironclads penetrated their defenses and moved upstream. In short, every dynasty and every phase of a dynasty touched upon naval matters. Even though they didn't build vast blue-water navies to colonize other countries, they did have extensive experience in building and using fleets. In fact, they were often the key to gaining or keeping power.[2]

GUNPOWDER ARMIES?

The Chinese are credited with being the first to discover and use firearms. Most popular knowledge assumes that the Chinese used them for little more than firecrackers, and it was the West that really perfected how to build and use gunpowder weapons. These assumptions are flawed in a couple of points. China knew how to build and use gunpowder weapons but their particular needs didn't lead to improved firearms or massed fire.[3]

The first mention of gunpowder comes from a Daoist text in the 800s. The earliest verified reference comes from the eleventh century. Chinese infantry used an early version of the formula for gunpowder to make a fire lance, a bamboo tube that essentially acted as a flamethrower or fire spear. These were direct ancestors of the firearm, as sometimes the Chinese would put small pebbles into the bamboo that would be discharged in the stream of fire. The first firearms as we know them were used in the mid-1100s, and by the time of the Ming dynasty, they were standard issue to the military and widely used.

But if the Chinese had firearms for so long, why did they fall behind the Europeans in their design and use? Like other military technology, such as crossbows, it has to do with a combi-

nation of geographic considerations and the type of threats the
Chinese faced. Early firearms were much less effective than is
commonly realized. They were incredibly slow to reload. In the
time it took an enemy to charge one hundred yards, a bowman
might be able to get off three shots, while somebody armed with
a musket could fire once. Reloading muskets was incredibly difficult, often involving a twenty-eight-step process, and for early
matchlock weapons it included holding a lit candle in one hand
and loading the gunpowder weapon with the other.[4] This, of
course, made them almost impossible to use on horseback. Intense training and massed fire helped to increase their rates of
fire and effectiveness, but even with massed fire, the bows had
a better firing rate and accuracy. Bows could be used on horseback, fired more often, and had better accuracy. For example,
eighteenth-century gunpowder weapons could hit a target thirty-
three yards wide at sixty-seven yards away only 50 percent of
the time (thirty-three yards wide is about the size of a good barn,
so they literally could only hit the broad side of a barn about
half the time).

The primary enemy of the Chinese was nomadic horse
archers. These armies were incredibly mobile, making it hard to
hit once with muskets, and they were able to achieve an incredible rate of fire. The slow rate of fire and inaccuracy made muskets a poor choice of weapon against nomads. It is no surprise
that China started to expand its power into the steppes during
the eighteenth century, when gunpowder weapons had much
better rates of fire and accuracy.

But the weapons were extremely good if you could mount
them on walls and ships. The wall or ship could support more-
effective and heavier weapons. Ships are much larger and slower
than horse archers, so they could be hit by gunpowder weapons.
The walls of town are even bigger than a ship and don't move
at all, so the Chinese developed very effective artillery. When
used against experienced Japanese forces (see chapter 9), those
forces reported that the ground shook. They were so effective
and unnerving that the Japanese tried to avoid direct engage-

ments with Chinese forces despite their superiority in small arms.

In contrast, European armies for the most part didn't face nomadic horse armies. They faced other groups of infantry. Much like the Chinese massing crossbow-equipped armies, the Europeans needed to mass more soldiers into an area and make sure they could fire, load, and reload in unison. They increasingly sought better and better weapons to the point that they eventually outclassed Chinese small-arms fire.

In short, the Chinese used gunpowder weapons far more than is commonly thought. They had different enemies and a unique set of circumstances that made small arms ineffectual. Because of the lack of incentives and poor effect in battle, they never developed new and better firearms. Instead, they developed rather good cannon mounted on ships and walls, and excellent siege artillery. They didn't show a cultural aversion to new weapons and didn't simply use gunpowder as fireworks. They actively imported the better small arms when they became aware of the difference late in the dynasty.

CONCLUSION

The Battle of Lake Poyang was a naval encounter that decisively established the Ming dynasty. It was one of the few times the south conquered the north. It established hundreds of years of Ming dynasty rule, and it suggests we should reassess our opinion of Chinese naval history and the country's use of gunpowder weapons. The next battle shows an example of Chinese gunpowder weapons in warfare, but it also shows those traditional Chinese values and military theory applied in the gunpowder age.

# THE SIEGE OF PYONGYANG

## 1593

Muskets are effective on wagons, on boats, and on foot. Recently a gun has been created that is fired on horseback. Firing a musket relies entirely on the priming powder. [Some may say:] When the horse gallops, which is how northerners are used to riding, if the priming powder is not spilled and scattered then it will be blown away by the wind, and then how will it fire? This is the talk of a person who does not know a lot about firearms. If it is a three eyed gun or one of the newly manufactured [pistol like] winged tiger guns, it can first be used as a gun and then after having been fired then it can serve as a hand to hand weapon. As for hitting the target and killing the enemy, I don't know.
—Zhao Shizen, writing in a sixteenth-century military manual

When the Japanese fire their muskets, you can still hear, even if they fire from all sides. But when the Chinese fire their cannon, the sky and the earth vibrates and the mountains and plains tremble and you can't even speak. . . . [M]ilitary affairs are simple. Big cannons defeat small cannons and many cannon defeat few cannon.

—Korean official, 1593

L I RUSONG'S CANNON SHOOK THE HEAVENS. The Japanese forces inside Pyongyang had yet to encounter that kind of resistance before. After unifying Japan and reportedly receiving a series of insults from China, Toyotomo Hideyoshi (1536–1598) had a large contingent of trained troops, excellent muskets, and a desire to change the world order in Asia. The Japanese invasion of Korea in 1592 launched what is popularly called the Imjin War, though many academic historians call it the First Sino-Japanese War of 1592–1598. The Japanese quickly overwhelmed the Koreans. They marched north and captured the pivotal city of Pyongyang and seemed poised to invade China through Manchuria. In response to the defeat of large parts of China's first expeditionary army and the flight of the Korean emperor to the Yalu River, the Wanli emperor (1563–1620) of the late Ming dynasty intervened to protect his vassal. At the time, the bulk of his available troops were dealing with a mutiny of a powerful frontier general centered in the northern Chinese city of Ningxia.

Li Rusong moved as quickly as he could across the northern frontier and across the Yalu River early in 1593. Upon entering Korea, and perhaps because of the time crunch, Li's army had only a modest amount of supplies. The army may have expected to receive additional supplies from the Koreans. If it did, Li possessed an unrealistic assumption based on incomplete intelligence. The army itself was reported to contain a good number of untrained conscripts with far fewer disciplined veterans, though they were eventually joined with some of the best-trained troops China could field, instructed by Qi Jiguang in the south. The lack of disciplined forces within Li's army could slow him down, as well as cause unnecessary casualties.

Li's forces seemed to lack the discipline to avoid Japanese intelligence gathering but also seemed to misread or ignore his intelligence concerning the inability of the Koreans to supplement Chinese supplies, the effects of terrain upon their cavalry forces, and the deadly disciplined fire of Japanese muskets. The Chinese heavy cannon proved difficult to move through the rough terrain of Korea, though they were invaluable in fighting against key cities and frightening Japanese forces.

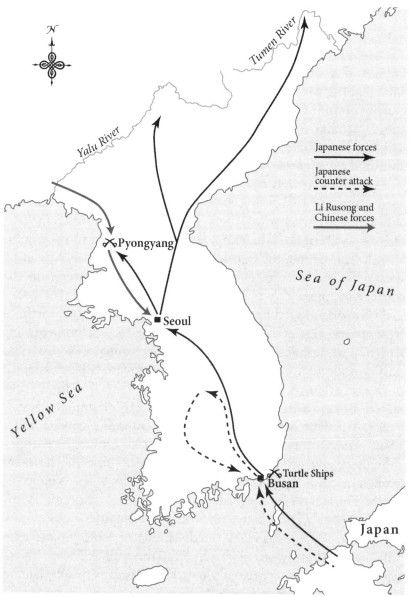

The Japanese Invasion of Korea, 1592. The Japanese invasion quickly overran the country before the decisive siege of Pyongyang. The Japanese retreated south, briefly led a second southern invasion indicated by the dotted line, before a peace treaty ended the conflict.

Likewise, the cavalry forces of the Chinese repeatedly bogged down in the muddy valleys they attempted to pass through. The snows froze the ground, but a thaw quickly produced soft ground that made cavalry operations and transporting cannon difficult. The first expeditionary army had been soundly defeated a year earlier because of this, and Li's horses later suffered the same fate, being ambushed a short time after the Siege of Pyongyang.

Li typically employed ruses to help his advance. One was to move toward Pyongyang under the guise of seeking a negotiation. On arriving close to the city, Li invited a Japanese delegation for what it thought was a parley. But instead of discussing matters, Li sprang a trap that sought to capture key leaders of the Japanese military. Some of the Japanese fought their way out of the ambush and managed to alert Japanese general Konishi Yukinaga at Pyongyang. Yukinaga dug into the city of Pyongyang and properly placed his forces to defend the city walls. Overall, the Japanese forces seemed more paralyzed by combat fatigue, sickness, and supply problems than by Chinese ruses.

The failure of Li's ruses left him with few options. He could outflank the Japanese position at Pyongyang, but the small army he possessed, the lack of supplies, and the difficulty of the terrain made an attack on Pyongyang the only option. While the Chinese had cannon that could blast in the walls during a siege, the Japanese had well-trained soldiers armed with muskets. The significant disadvantages of muskets are negated behind a fortification, and their advantages are increased. Thus, many nations, the Japanese included, adopted the fortified wagon approach to allow their gunpowder forces proper cover as they reloaded; the cover offered by fortifications made the enemy approach into the muskets' effective range and sometimes even funneled the enemy into a deadly enfilade of small-arms fire.

In approaching Pyongyang, Li needed to clear the hilltop fort just to the north of the city. This secured his flank and protected its rear as Chinese forces attacked. Perhaps conserving the strength of his troops, or maybe taking advantage of a displaced people, he attacked with Korean warrior monks. After taking the hill and softening the city with his cannon, Li begin the frontal assault on the city proper with a feint attack from the south. At the same time, Li personally led an attack from the west. He then used incendiary attacks to mask his attack against the city. While the fire effectively masked the advance of Li toward the city, the postbattle analysis revealed that the use of fire could have burned the grass and stores needed to feed the Chinese cavalry. The fire attacks and smoke from cannon and musket fire, on top of the opening phase of the battle, added to the chaos. The indiscriminate use of cannon fire and incendiary attacks belied the fact that the Chinese were liberating a major Korean city. The city was already in ruinous condition before the battle, and the withering artillery fire made it even worse for the returning Koreans.

As his army began to falter outside the city walls, Li personally shot the first man who fled and then offered a reward to the first man to scale the wall. Once the walls had been breached, in the chaos of the city fighting, many of Li's troops beheaded anybody they could find. The system of rewards (beyond the special one instituted by Li in front of the gates) was based on the number of heads a soldier could present as evidence of his effectiveness in combat. The Japanese tried to break out from the southwest against the supposedly unreliable Korean forces. Those forces turned out to be Chinese in disguise; according to sources, this caused the Japanese to retreat back into the city in a panic.

After bitter hand-to-hand fighting and witnessing the effect of cannon fire on their fortifications, the Japanese were ready to attempt a second retreat from the city. The fortifications were breached, and they faced encirclement. Korean writers claimed that Li accepted a bribe, thus allowing the Japanese to cross the Taedong River unmolested. Other accounts suggest that the Japanese retreated under the cover of darkness across the frozen river. Whatever happened, Li did not follow up his victory at Pyongyang with an immediate pursuit of the enemy. He may have been short on supplies.

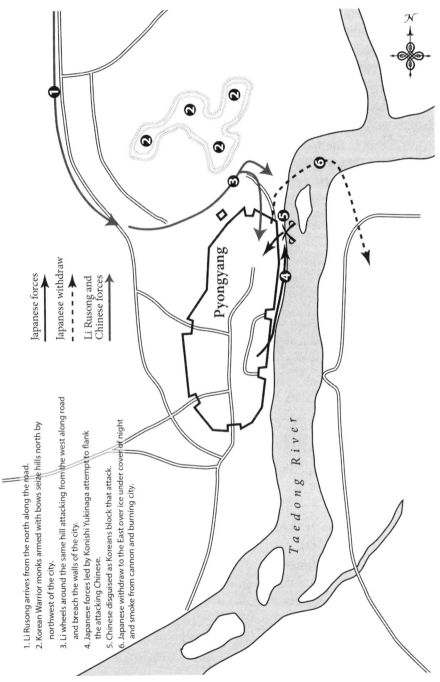

1. Li Rusong arrives from the north along the road.
2. Korean Warrior monks armed with bows seize hills north by northwest of the city.
3. Li wheels around the same hill attacking from the west along road and breach the walls of the city.
4. Japanese forces led by Konishi Yukinaga attempt to flank the attacking Chinese.
5. Chinese disguised as Koreans block that attack.
6. Japanese withdraw to the East over ice under cover of night and smoke from cannon and burning city.

Japanese forces

Japanese withdraw

Li Rusong and Chinese forces

Pyongyang

Taedong River

The Siege of Pyongyang, 1593.

After a short break, Li did pursue the fleeing Japanese forces. Eventually the conflict settled down around the southern end of the peninsula as peace talks slowly progressed. The war is mostly known in Korea because of the national icon Yi Sun Sin. He led spiked ships called turtle boats, which decimated the much larger Japanese fleet and made resupply of its army in Korea very difficult. The other factors that led to an end of the war included the death of Hideyoshi, who commanded the invasion; the defeat of a follow-up force later in the decade; and continuing guerrilla warfare from Korean forces.[1] The peace treaty proved effective enough to end the conflict.

## LATE MING DYNASTY

The general perception among scholars is that the late Ming dynasty was one of decline. Viewed through the lens of the dynastic cycle, it had entered its death throes. But the campaigns of the Wanli emperor decisively show that it was not in complete decline. During a period of ten years in the late sixteenth and early seventeenth centuries, the Ming campaigned and won in every corner of the empire. Some allied northwestern tribes of Mongols rebelled and were swiftly crushed. Li Rusong was then directed to Korea. There the Ming dynasty successfully defended its vassal against a much larger and experienced Japanese force that was closer to its supply lines. Finally, the Ming defeated rebelling tribesmen in the remote southwest. The Ming dynasty overcame vast logistical challenges and severe threats, including the dynasty's extensive and successful counterinsurgency against the Wokou, or dwarf pirates, along the southeastern coast.

The martial success across its empire shows how the Ming retained what modern analysts would call strong fundamentals. They had a large population, a good tax base, increasing wealth, and a military that was large and fairly well-equipped. The problems in this era, and a cause of decline, emanated from bureaucratic inertia. The chief ministers fought among themselves and with the eunuchs who advised the emperor. A vigorous military leader and strong emperor could cut through the red tape to promote good policies and make good military decisions. But most emperors toward the end of the Ming dynasty looked at the infighting among their ministers and voluminous reports generated by the government apparatus and simply stopped caring. After all, they were emperors and could live a life of luxury in any number of opulent palaces as they pursued their favorite hobbies. The various regional governors and local officials managed their territories reasonably well, but what we would call national, foreign, and domestic policy generally became listless.

In short, much like the collapse of the Song dynasty described in chapter 7, a lack of strong leadership and proper military policy led to weakness in the late Ming dynasty. A strong leader could direct the proper military and economic resources to a certain region, conduct diplomacy, and properly harness the strong military families like the Li.

Another group whose talents were properly harnessed in the late Ming dynasty was the Qi clan. The most famous member of the clan, Qi Jiguang (1528–1588), was born into a hereditary military family. He recruited, trained, equipped, and led Chinese forces against Japanese pirates from 1555–1565 and is credited by historians with ending their threat.[2] Qi's writings, *The New Book Recording Effective Techniques* and the *Record of Military Training*, evoked a system of rewards and punishments discussed in the Seven Military Classics by theorists such as Sunzi and Wuzi to create disciplined armies.

One of Qi's unique creations was called the Mandarin Duck Formation. It consisted of an eleven-person unit led by a squad leader with two teams of five: one multiple-tipped-spear person to entangle the enemy weapon (because the pirates often fought in the littorals of the south, this was usually a melee weapon designed for close-quarters combat), one shield person to protect him, two spear people to assist in thrusting at the enemy trying to untangle his weapon, and one sword person for additional combat power. Qi directed that squads repeatedly drill in coordinating their individual and mutually supportive functions. While the function of individual members remained the same, the specific configuration could be changed between three models. Soldiers who faced different types of enemies, such as nomadic horsemen and regular Chinese infantry, benefitted from Qi's disciplinary guidelines and grappling techniques. In fact, Li Rusong credited Qi's teaching for the "total victory" of the Chinese forces in the Sino-Japanese War and specifically praised the southern troops in his theater. The Koreans were so impressed with the skill of Chinese soldiers trained with these methods that they trained exclusively from Qi's manual for much of the seventeenth century.

LEADERSHIP QUALITIES

Qi's training material explicitly borrowed from a vast Chinese heritage. This gives us a chance to examine more closely how the Siege of Pyongyang might illustrate the continued influence of and possible changes to classical military theory in the gunpowder age. The methods and applications of Qi were one example of this, and another was Li's leadership in Korea.

Li was censured by Confucian officials during the early years of his career for licentiousness and later for inattention to proper military discipline, mismanagement of military affairs, and raising his hands at his civil counterparts. Of those charges, the first seems to be the most serious. Tai Kong, in the Seven Military Classics, taught that the ruler (and by extension his generals) must cultivate values like benevolence, righteousness, loyalty, credibility, sincerity, courage, and wisdom. Many of these values have utilitarian purposes, such as courage to inspire soldiers during difficult moments in a campaign.

The other charges had dangerous implications as well, yet their potential political causes make them suspect. Civil servants, jealous and fearful of military success and the increasing strength of military households, could easily trump up charges against Li. In fact, historians suggest this in their study of the Li family, and the charges are similar to those faced by the Wu family in the thirteenth century. Li Rusong's later actions proved his courage and desire to faithfully defend Chinese interests.[3]

Tactically, Li's actions during the siege of Ningxia and other skirmishes against the rebels establish a baseline that can be applied to his later actions in Korea. The Li family is reported to have excelled at ambushes, forced marches, and night attacks with the intent of confusing their foes. Upon the failure of his ruse, he progressed with a standard siege, although one could interpret his actions as pinning the enemy in place with an orthodox siege and then attempting to strike the killing blow with unorthodox tactics. If true, this attempt mirrors one of the central and most unique concepts in Chinese military theory, where a combination of orthodox and unorthodox tactics served to pin an enemy in place, preparing it for a devastating blow from unorthodox tactics.[4] In Li's case, he followed his siege of the rebellious city of Ningxia with a daring night attack and then flooded the land around the city, cutting it off from reinforcements. Finally, he dangled bogus offers of clemency to encourage fighting within the enemy's ranks. These unconventional measures were interspersed with conventional frontal attacks that, although led courageously by Li, caused great suffering and casualties among his forces and did little to take the city. They also left openings for the enemy to conduct its own raids on his camps.

Upon defeating the rebels, Li turned his attention to the situation in Korea. From sources it appears that he prepared what he thought was the proper amount of supplies for his expedition. This reflects the admonition of Sunzi to employ the military only after the ruler has gathered the necessary supplies.[5] Sunzi also stressed the need for proper mental preparation, yet the Ming civil and military leaders seem to have acted in ignorance of proper intelligence. In making their initial estimations, the Ming ignored the signs of an imminent invasion of one of their tributaries, perhaps the same way they ignored the growing signs of rebellion in Ningxia. Then, after the invasion, they misread the intelligence, and some even assumed the Koreans were actively aiding the Japanese in their conquest. The first expedition ignored the warning of the Koreans about the deadly disciplined fire of Japanese muskets. After that expedition's defeat, Li Rusong seemed to ignore the same warnings concerning Japanese musketeers.

Li used ruses in front of the city. He turned the parley with Japanese diplomatic officials into an ambush out of which the Japanese forces fought. This closely matches one of Sunzi's greatest themes: "warfare is the way of deception." He adds that "when such deception is imaginatively created and effectively implemented, the enemy will neither know where to attack nor what formations to employ and thus be condemned to making fatal errors."[6] In this case, the Japanese generals seemed unfazed by Chinese machinations.

The ineffectiveness of Li's deception could mean two things. First, it could have resulted from the lack of discipline among Li's forces. Second, the Japanese were resistant to this form of warfare because they were close neighbors with a long history of fighting the same foes and each other. In a sense, the Japanese could fight fire with fire and thus did not get burned by Chinese manipulations. Plus, the Japanese forces were known for their discipline, so they had the presence of mind to fight their way out of Li's ambush and perceive possible deception in his peace overtures, and they planned accordingly.

The battle itself presents numerous lessons for study, including the proper use of soldiers respective to the terrain, the use of rewards and punishments during the fight, the ability to lead from the front and lead through hardships, the ruse of using what appeared to be Korean troops, using incendiary attacks, the lack of harmonious conduct by the troops, and the question of whether superior numbers, and not superior leadership, won the battle for Li.

In the desperate moments before the city walls, Li seemed to rely on the classic Chinese technique of instilling discipline through rewards and punishments: "if by executing one man the entire army will quake, kill him. If by rewarding one man the masses will be pleased, reward him . . . [T]hen your awesomeness has been effected."[7] The command for rewards and punishments comes from the Legalist tradition, where only a strong centralized state could survive among warring factions.

This could represent what the Chinese call higher and lower forms of combat and signify important connections to Daoist notions of harmony in Chinese thought. Political scientist Alastair Johnson argued that Chinese thought held what he called the Confucian Mencius view. One of the prominent beliefs included the idea that the righteousness and good governance of a ruler could prevent conflict.[8] Confucian historians considered the resort to warfare as an admission of the ruler's moral bankruptcy.[9]

Sunzi frequently referred to flowing water to describe a victorious army. For example, "the combat of the victorious is like the sudden release of a pent up torrent down a thousand fathom gorge."[10] The lowest form of combat consisted of bloody attacks against fortified positions. The actions of Li during the Korean campaign consisted of an ambush that might seem dastardly to modern Western readers but actually represented an attempt to avoid lower forms of combat that resulted in costly battles that killed large numbers of soldiers and devastated cities.

Rewards and punishments, leading from the front, and fire attacks won the battle and eventually the war, but they took the lives of many Koreans and made life incredibly difficult for the ones who survived. This stands in stark contrast to the ruler's supposed purpose in going to war. Tai Kong taught that a ruler (and by extension his generals) should lead with Confucian values of benevolence and virtue with policies that benefit the average man. This would bind the people in loving harmony with their ruler and allow him to recruit the motivated populace into his army. This also represented the harmonious goal of many classic writers. Under Daoist influence, many writers viewed war as an evil but necessary last resort in order to restore harmony to the realm. While winning the battle would seem to fulfill the goal of restoring order, the suffering of the Korean population perpetrated by their supposed protectors seemed to lead to great friction between the civilian population and the ruling dynasty. It also led to greater friction between Korean and Chinese leaders. So instead of restoring harmony through a higher form of battle, Li escalated tensions through the lower form.

Contemporary Korean historians accuse Li of being bribed or possibly being unable to exploit his victory at Pyongyang. A final explanation or Li's sluggish pace after his victory could reflect the maze of mirrors that accompanied Asian warfare. For instance, Sunzi said that "if the enemy opens the door, you must race in."[11] Yet a charging army could be entering an ambush and trap. The pursuing Chinese forces were in fact ambushed at Pyokje a short time after the Siege of Pyongyang. Li might not have started an immediate pursuit because he wanted to reassess his strength after a battle, reorder his forces, check supplies, and then proceed at a pace that would decrease the chance of an ambush. (Since he was in fact ambushed during his pursuit south, his caution seems warranted.) This may have seemed dilatory to anxious Korean officials and could even be condemned through a close reading of Chinese military theorists, but Li could also point to various considerations and classical theory as well to support his cautious pause.

After a brief period (that was annoyingly long to the Koreans), Li moved with great haste against the remaining Japanese forces. But he failed to properly take into account the terrain he was moving through and was ambushed along a narrow valley during early spring. The valley allowed the Japanese to quickly close and engage in hand-to-hand combat, while the early spring had thawed the road into a muddy mess. This negated the Chinese advantage in cavalry and combat power and played into the superior ability of Japanese small-arms and melee combat. Only the timely intervention of Li's remaining force prevented total disaster.

Even though Li seemed to operate with a great deal of faithfulness to classic texts, his actions also differed a great deal. There is no word about gunpowder in the thousand-year-old writings. Thus cannon fire would make a siege better for Chinese forces. Gunpowder weapons— except for the relatively new pistols, or what they called three-eyed guns—were ineffective on horseback. And Chinese writers even advised that after firing a pistol, it should be used as a bludgeon. Qi Jiguang trained his infantry in close-order formations that didn't include gunpowder weapons. Chinese military writings often have disputed translations, interpretations, and contested authenticity of their authors. The Confucian officials writing the histories were often more concerned with enhancing their position at the expense of uncouth military men. If they did include an example of Chinese military theory, it was because they wanted to show how book learning could lead to success on the battlefield, and probably not that the general actually followed theory. One late Ming dynasty specialist, for example, argued that the Seven Military Classics were hardly used during the Ming dynasty. Citations of those works were so rare that he noted the exceptions. The Kangxi Emperor (1654–1722), one of the most powerful martial leaders in Chinese history, famously called the Seven Military Classics "worthless."[12]

That said, Qi Jiguang's military manual included large amounts of material that recalled classic writers. One could argue that Chinese values and their ways of war were so ingrained that they didn't need to specifically mention it. Anybody with passing familiarity with the classics could notice a similarity between Li's use of rewards and punishments in front of the walls of Pyongyang and the instructions in the classics. It is clear, then, that Chinese forces were at least partially influenced by the military classics, as they still acted in several clear ways according to its principles and consciously copied them in their written works, even though gunpowder weapons affected the practice of warfare in this age.

CONCLUSION

The Siege of Pyongyang represented one of the most pivotal battles in one of the largest conflicts in modern East Asian history. It is even called the first regional war, in comparison to the latter one that was a part of World War II. The fight shows the continuing strength of the late Ming dynasty and helps to dispel the notion that it was bound to decline as part of an artificial dynastic cycle. The application of the classic military theories was more nuanced than typically thought. Li Rusong and Qi Jiguang likely used inherited ideas and cultural values from Sunzi and other classic writers, but there was a great deal of variance from them in accordance with new technology. Some leaders disregarded the classic teachings, while others consciously and effectively modeled their writings on them. The application of ancient principles in dangerous modern times applied even more when British ships arrived at their doorstep during the next war.

# 10

# THE BATTLE OF ZHENJIANG

## 1842

You O King, are so inclined toward our civilization that you have sent a special envoy across the seas to bring to our Court your memorial of congratulations on the occasion of my birthday and to present your native products as an expression of your thoughtfulness. On perusing your memorial, so simply worded and sincerely conceived I am impressed by your genuine respectfulness and friendliness and greatly pleased. . . . The Celestial Court has pacified and possessed the territory within the four seas. Its sole aim is to do its utmost to achieve good government and to manage political affairs, attaching no value to strange jewels and precious objects. The various articles presented by you, O King, this time are accepted by my special order to the office in charge of such functions in consideration of the offerings having come from a long distance with sincere good wishes. As a matter of fact, the virtue and prestige of the Celestial Dynasty having spread far and wide, the kings of the myriad nations come by land and sea with all sorts of precious things. Consequently there is nothing we lack, as your principal envoy and others have themselves observed. We have never set much store on strange or ingenious objects, nor do we need any more of your country's manufactures.
                    —Emperor Qian Long to England, 1793

A survey of all the states in the world will show that those states that undertook reforms became strong while those states that clung to the past perished. . . . Our present trouble lies in our clinging to old institutions without knowing how to change. In an age of competition between states, to put into effect methods appropriate to an era of universal unification and laissez-faire is like wearing heavy furs in the summer or riding a high carriage across a river. . . . It is a principle of things that the new is strong but the old is weak. . . . Moreover, our present institutions are but the unworthy vestiges of the Han, Tang, Yuan, and the Ming dynasties. . . . In fact, they are the products of the fancy writing and corrupt dealing of petty officials rather than the original ideas of the ancestors. . . . After studying ancient and modern institutions, Chinese and foreign, I have found that the institutions of the sage kings and the Three Dynasties [of Xia, Shang, and Zhou] were excellent, but that ancient times were different from today. . . . I beg Your Majesty to adopt the purpose of Peter the Great of Russia as our purpose and to take the Meiji Reform of Japan as the model of our reform.

—Kang Youwei, *Comprehensive Consideration of the Whole Situation*

THE CAPITAL AT BEIJING was in a precarious position. Even though British forces were still hundreds of miles away and their naval forces couldn't land enough infantry to fight there, the British were close enough to the Grand Canal at Zhenjiang to cut the grain supply to Beijing. Since the sixth century Sui dynasty rulers built the canal, it had been a vital logistical line that fed Beijing and the other capitals of the north.

About nine thousand soldiers and eight thousand Manchu Bannermen of the Qing dynasty fought outside the gate. After bitter fighting, the bannermen were forced back into the city. The British disembarked their heavy cannon and blasted the north gate. Still, the bannermen resisted at the gate. The British brought special scaling ladders, and the bannermen fought on the palisades. They fought in the streets, and the bodies piled up. After a lengthy stuggle, and over 1,500 British deaths, they secured the city. The British had cut the vital lifeline to the court at Beijing, and peace negotiations started.

The Chinese had banned opium almost fifty years before but hardly enforced the ban. There was even a thriving homegrown industry in the Sichuan valley. But the trade imbalance with the British over this product produced friction for both parties. Lin Zexu, the local governor of the trade city of Guangzhou (called Canton by the British), became increasingly strident as he tried to enforce the ban. The British leader of the naval forces, Charles Elliot, and other British officials were annoyed at the sudden restrictions being placed on them. Things came to a head in 1839, when Lin demanded that the British hand over all the opium in port and sign additional agreements in order to trade, but Elliot wouldn't oblige. They resented the infringement of their rights as British men and free traders. The Chinese then moved war junks, small ships armed with cannon, to a position where they could fire on the British ships.

This led to the first battle in late 1839. In response to being denied free trade, the British war vessels closed the entire port to trade. By November 1839, one of the British merchant vessels tried to run the blockade. Thirteen Manchu junks and sixteen fire boats prevented British ships from firing on their rogue trader. After a furious but inconclusive firefight, the British ships disengaged. Because the British withdrew, Lin enhanced his role, and the outcome of the battle was a victory that he dutifully reported to the emperor. A tense standoff continued through much of 1840, as the British widened their blockade around southern coastal cities and negotiations faltered. The Chinese were ready to force the British ships away from Macao, but the British preempted them. This in turn led to the Battle of the Barrier, in which a combination of disembarked British marines and devastating naval fire from corvettes destroyed the barrier separating the trading port of Macao from the entrance to China.

At this point, the British wanted to force a conclusion to the conflict but couldn't move on Beijing. They could, however, cut the Grand Canal and attempt to starve the emperor into submission. The British assembled a force almost nine thousand

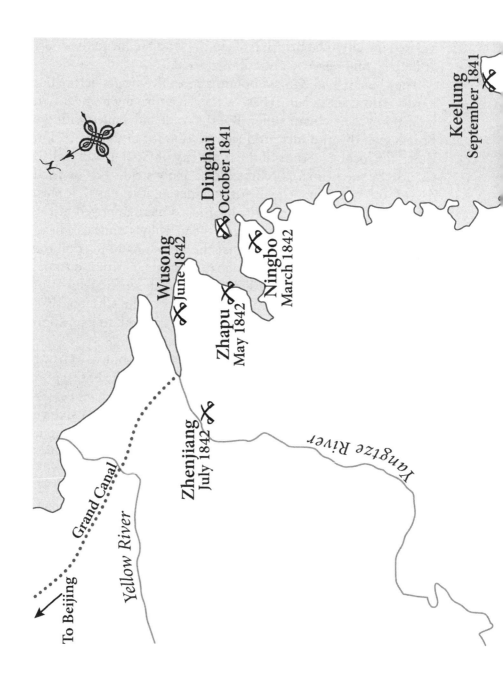

Keelung
September 1841

Dinghai
October 1841

Ningbo
March 1842

Wusong
June 1842

Zhapu
May 1842

Zhenjiang
July 1842

Yangtze River

Grand Canal

Yellow River

To Beijing

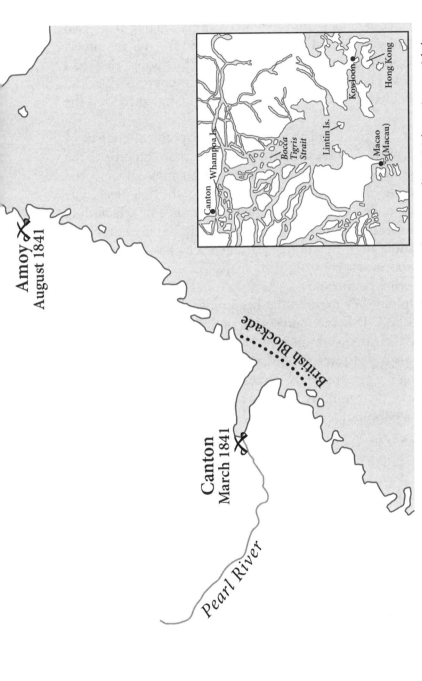

The First Opium War, 1839–1842. Each of these battles was a British victory, but since the British at times withdrew after doing the most damage, Qing general Lin Zexu would report them as Chinese victories to the court, leading to a dangerous sense of complacency by Qing rulers.

strong, which included about eighteen ships ranging from two seventy-four-gun men of war to a half dozen frigates to numerous corvettes and smaller vessels. Up until this point, they had fought local Han troops. After bypassing numerous river defenses and coastal forts, they reached Zhenjiang and seized the city.

The loss of grain and increasing loss of political control of territories south of Yangtze brought the Chinese emperor to the bargaining table. The resulting Treaty of Nanjing underscored the free-trade issues that drove the conflict in the first place. The British demanded the Chinese open five trade cities, including Guangzhou and Shanghai. The treaty stipulated that Hong Kong become an open and free port. (The city had only recently returned to Chinese control.) Britain also gained any concessions made to other countries.

The Opium War marked the beginning of a century of Chinese weakness. This was a pivotal period in Chinese history that witnessed their first sustained interaction with and defeat by the West. It also illustrates several important myths and realities concerning the perception of Chinese military weakness, the performance of their military, and the attempts at importing Western military technology.

MYTHS AND REALITY

The battles of the Opium War were hardly more than skirmishes in many cases, especially compared to later conflicts like the Taiping rebellion or China's war against Japanese aggression during World War II. But it still had a prodigious impact on Chinese society and led to the creation of several myths that obscure how Chinese leaders grappled with modernization. Probably the myth with the most cultural impact comes from Chinese historiography. Chinese textbooks still start modern history sections with the Opium War and label it the first of many examples of greedy foreign conquest.

The history books turn Lin into a nationalist hero for his anti-imperialist stance, even though his intransigence likely contributed to the conflict. In fact, the first battle featured a British merchant vessel being fired on by British warships protected by Chinese warships. The insistence on open cities for commerce in the peace treaty points more toward the British desire for free trade and not a desire to unfairly extract resources from China. Though it is called the first of the "unequal" treaties by Chinese scholars, the Nanjing Treaty that ended the war actually benefitted the local Han Chinese at the expense of the Qing dynasty's Manchu court. It restored rights regarding free trade that the Han felt they had lost to a conquest dynasty. Lin's writings indicate that he hated Chinese merchants and thought they were evil, while the British were just his opponents. The ethnic Han witnesses to the Battle of Zhenjiang disliked the Manchus to the point that they were ambivalent about British victory or defeat.[1]

The British had the good fortune, then, that allowed them to exploit ethnic divisions within Chinese society that would flower into rebellion and a collapse of the Qing dynasty in the next seventy years. This, combined with other factors we will see, increased the British impression of easy victories against an inferior foe. In the Battle of Chuanbi, the British tactically withdrew, which led Lin Zexu to declare a victory. At what historians now call the Sanyuanli Incident, named for the minor village near Guangzhou, local militia surrounded an isolated attachment of British soldiers, caused minor casualties, and made the British withdraw. This led to another report of victory, which contributed to an unwarranted sense of complacency in the Qing court. The court should have instead been wondering why a force outnumbered ten to one could not only survive but withdraw with minimal casualties. But the Qing amply rewarded individuals for victory, which incentivized exaggerating and outright lying. This led to reports that were then called the "Six Smashing Victories" in the Opium War.

Another contributing factor to China's loss resulted from Confucian officials who labeled the British pirates or invaders. The incorrect labels from officials made the local administrators recall the Japanese dwarf pirates of the sixteenth century. (That conflict also featured disputes over trade rights between local southern merchants and the officials in the capital.) Because of this label, Chinese leaders adopted a somewhat passive stance that had worked well against invaders and pirates in the past, believing that all they had to do was defend with enough force to make plundering unattractive. This ceded the initiative to the British and made the Chinese forces seem rather weak in their passivity. It also aided British objectives, as they could dictate strategy and apply pressure at just the right points not to plunder but to force policy changes that would aid free trade. The Han forces weren't very motivated to fight and often retreated early in a battle. The British freedom of action and low casualties gave them a sense of a one-sided fight, but they faced ethnic Han who disliked the Manchu and fought a passive strategy dictated by incorrectly applying historical experience.

The Chinese had impressive numbers of ships with fairly advanced equipment and tactics. British leaders in Guangzhou, for example, worried that the large number of Chinese junks could overwhelm them. The junks were armed with cannon comparable in size to what the British had, though they had trouble aiming them. At the Battle of Chuanbi, for example, the British soldiers reported that with better aiming, the Chinese could have raked the decks of British ships and caused far more damage. Later in the war the British faced Manchu Bannermen. Unlike the Han defenders, they were strictly loyal to the dynasty and were well-trained and equipped. This resulted in the intense Battle of Zhenjiang, where British forces suffered heavy casualties and faced a stiff challenge.

The difference in the Opium War turned out to be the British edge in technology. But it was a small edge and only began the year the war started. The original ships in the region were subject to the winds and currents. Just as at the Battle of Lake Poyang, this meant they had trouble moving upriver in narrow spaces because it opened them up to fire attacks. But the new ironclad *Nemesis* was different. It was only completed the year the war started. Its steam-powered engine left the ship unaffected by the wind. Its hull was constructed in six segments, which meant that if one was penetrated by cannon or rocks, which happened at several points in the conflict, it wouldn't sink. The most effective advantage was its shallow draft of only six feet. The steam-powered ships were relatively well-armed, with two thirty-two-pound guns and six six-pounders, and the small draft meant they could navigate previously unnavigable rivers. During the Opium War, the British penetrated small creeks near Guangzhou that were as shallow as four-and-a-half feet. According to reports, at some points the river was so shallow the *Nemesis* practically slithered along the mud. This allowed British forces to outflank naval fortifications positioned to stop vessels operating in deep water, not powerful ships operating in shallow water. The relatively advanced Chinese fortresses were rendered useless, and the British could attack places that were often undefended and do so from unexpected directions. The Chinese adapted during the war as well. They started using pivot mounts on junks and fielding their own gunboats. But the reports of Chinese victories and the belief that they could simply outlast what the officials mislabeled as pirates meant it was too little too late. Combined with the previously described apathy of Han soldiers, the shallow-draft ironclads gave the British a war-winning advantage.

This wasn't a case of cavalry charging tanks, or spearmen charging machine-gun nests. The Chinese forces in the previous century had used gunpowder weapons and railroads to advance farther than any other dynasty. The longest ruling and most martially accomplished emperors, such as the Kangxi and Qianlong emperors, collectively reigned for over one hundred years. They left a peaceful, strong, and expanded empire protected by a strong military armed with relatively modern weapons and a healthy amount of money in their treasury. Their country's population, if not their territory, dwarfed that of just about any other nation on Earth, and the Qianlong emperor had only died about forty years before the Opium War. But the latter years of his reign witnessed the beginning of protracted ethnic rebellions from the Muslim minorities, which drained the treasury. It also presaged the problems that China would face in the nineteenth

Imperialism in China, 1824–1924.

century with frequent rebellions and a military increasingly unable to quell them.

So at the start of the Opium War, the Chinese had well-trained armies with advanced weaponry. There was some local variation, of course, but it was still an impressive empire with a large military, tax base, and territory under its control. It was a specific set of circumstances—ranging from ethnic tension between the ruling Manchu and ethnic Han to unwise policy choices based on a misreading of British intentions to new technology—that defeated China. It was hardly the backward East being overawed by European strength, as many people believe. This was a devastating and shocking defeat for China, but it was due to specific historical events and conditions, not Eastern aversion to technology or insurmountable Western superiority.

SELF-STRENGTHENING

The Chinese reactions to their defeat during the Opium War were largely based on cultural and political considerations. Because the Manchus were not ethnically Han, they feared any reforms in the army could be used against them. (The mutiny of armies which ended up being reformed did contribute to their downfall in 1911.) The Manchus could also point to victory reports received and blame defeats on incompetent Han troops. The Manchus were keenly aware of, and their Confucian officials never let them forget, their obligations as good Confucian rulers. Sadly, the one lesson not learned from the conflict was the need to modernize; it was another twenty years until the recovery from the near death blow during the Taiping Rebellion of the 1860s that Chinese rulers pursued establishing modern, gunpowder-equipped armies.

Chinese victories for the half century after the Opium War showed evidence of the Manchu's adaptability and strength. Chinese armies equipped with Western-style rifles and tactics recovered from shocks and setbacks, and even expanded farther into central Asia. They fought a brief war and resolved the conflict with Russia over the pivotal Ili valley and province. They subdued the Taiping Rebellion and defeated Muslim-led revolts in the remote Yunnan Province. Just like the Wanli emperor in the late Ming dynasty (see chapter 9), this period proved that an active and capable leader could still secure and recover territory, as well as make modest improvements in adopting Western arms. Compared to the collapse of the Song and Ming dynasties, the Qing government did a capable job against stronger threats in creating peace and prosperity.[2]

While the Chinese were able to respond to land-based threats and internal rebellions very well, the European naval threats to areas that were nominally under their control were a different story. They fought and lost two wars against the British, which prompted improvements in technology research and acquisition of more-advanced martial technology, as well as in educating soldiers to effectively use it.[3] But they lost two more pivotal wars in the latter decades of the century, which showed that their efforts at modernizing were still halting and inadequate. They fought the Sino-French War in 1883–1885 for control of the Gulf of Tonkin and the territory we now know as Vietnam. The war highlighted some of the larger trends in this period that made self-strengthening difficult. The efforts at military reform were led by various local leaders in a very inconsistent and political fashion. Li Hongzhang (1823–1901) was considered one of the leading reform advocates in the 1870s. He governed a pivotal central Chinese province and led soldiers to subdue the Taiping and Muslim revolts. He and several other governors were rewarded with great autonomy because of their loyalty and relatively successful efforts at modernizing. But he and the other reformers had a tough time deciding on which European country they should model their new fleet, and he argued with many of the other leading advocates for reform. Both of these factors meant that even when the court committed to reform, it was done in a haphazard way. The result was modern ships and armies that lacked standardized equipment and spare parts. This was a common theme until the end of World War II, as China at various points in this period obtained Soviet, German, Japanese, American, British, and French advisers and equipment. Sometimes it obtained parts and equipment from multiple countries at the same time.

Assuming they did have working equipment, doctrine and training was still very uneven. (See chapter 11 for a discussion of military doctrine.) Even with the best equipment, China didn't always apply it in a conflict, because of factional infighting, and didn't use it properly in combat. Once the conflict with France began, Li Hongzhang didn't allow his northern Chinese fleet to move south. He jealously procured and guarded the very best ships (ironically, French built) and didn't want to risk losing them. As in the Opium War, though, the Chinese performance wasn't such a clear-cut failure. They scored several victories over French infantry in northern Vietnam, and ended up losing control of only a small amount of territory on the periphery that became the French colony of Vietnam.

They had performed better, but their efforts were still not enough. It was the First Sino-Japanese War in 1894–1895 that clearly revealed Chinese weakness and signaled the beginning of the end for the dynasty. The conduct of China's army and sea forces were a complete embarrassment for the Qing dynasty and its Manchu rulers. Their army was sent retreating back to China, with core Chinese territory penetrated, and Beijing was close to falling. Despite having superior numbers, the navy was destroyed. Once again, the northern and southern Chinese navies failed to assist each other, but it likely wouldn't have helped. The Japanese fleet completely outmaneuvered, outperformed, and annihilated the much larger Chinese fleet. The resulting treaty removed Korea and Taiwan from the Chinese orbit and subjected China to years of Japanese aggression. Many local Japanese leaders regularly seized territory and created puppet states to advance their careers. In 1931, the Japanese staged the "Mukden Incident" in which they blamed Chinese insurgents for attempting to destroy a Japanese-owned railway in China. The incident gave the Japanese pretense to invade Manchuria and establish the puppet state of Manchukuo, in what many historians consider to be the true start of World War II.

After the First Sino-Japanese War, Germany, Russia, and Great Britain demanded additional trade concessions in Chinese ports, the rights to use railroads, and special protections for missionaries. Concessions to America were smaller but still con-

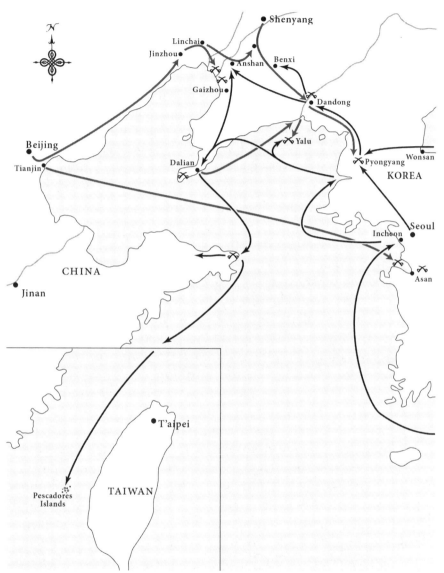

The First Sino-Japanese War, 1894–1895. Japan quickly marched its forces north, and defeated the larger Chinese army at Asan outside of Seoul. Japanese forces continued to pursue and defeat Chinese forces at Pyongyang and the Yalu River. At the same time the Japanese fleet smashed the Chinese ships in Yalu Bay, the Japanese invaded Manchuria and seized the Pescadores islands off the coast of Taiwan. Chinese rulers sued for peace and Japan was granted Korea, Taiwan, and the Liaodong Peninsula with its key port of Dalian. The port was renamed Port Arthur when the peninsula was returned to China and leased by Russia.

sisted of the Open Door Policy that allowed American goods to flood China. In short, the First Sino-Japanese War revealed the ineffectiveness of the Manchus in the face of Western nations. It wasn't because of an aversion to Western technology or China being an incredibly backward nation but, arguably, because of unique circumstances that made reforms incredibly halting and uneven.

In addition to the provincial governors, the leading Confucian scholars of this period often made uneven efforts at reform. Traditional Confucian interpretations dominated until the Taiping Rebellion. The Manchu rulers were starting to see the beginning of various ethnic rebellions from Han Chinese and Muslims. The rebels armed with modern weapons caused as many as sixty million casualties, and the success of the court in suppressing them solidified the Manchu's rule enough to justify self-strengthening. Prominent Confucian officials and the Manchu court believed that the essence of Confucianism remained the same, but what they called useful contrivances could be borrowed from the West.

After the Manchu's disastrous defeat at the hands of the Japanese, the essence/borrowing method—where the essence of Confucian philosophy remained unchanged, while useful or needed ideas from the West could be borrowed—seemed inadequate, and leading scholars such as Kang Youwei (1858–1927), quoted at the beginning of this chapter, began to reinterpret the essence of Confucianism and argued that Confucius was a reformer and Confucianism a policy of change. This policy lasted until 1911 with the collapse of the Qing dynasty. With the end of the last dynasty, and particularly after World War I, leading Chinese thinkers began to abandon Confucianism and embrace Western ideas. During this period, ideas were judged and adopted based on their ability to help solve Chinese problems. This phase is often called the May Fourth Movement, after an incident in Beijing on May 4, 1919, where thousands of demonstrators marched to protest the Treaty of Versailles, which awarded former German territory in China to Japan. This affront created strong nationalistic feelings, and thousands of demonstrators merged with reform-minded advocates. This movement also coincided with the rise of warlords and allowed the Chinese people and leaders to experiment with new ideologies such as communism and nationalism.

The leaders of this movement were Cai Yuanpei (1868–1940), who became the chancellor at Beijing University, and Chen Duxiu (1879–1942), who became his dean of letters. They made the university a haven for scholars fleeing the chaos of China or returning from study abroad. Their nationalistic and anti-imperialistic ideas spread quickly to the rest of China, and especially to other scholars in urban centers. After the slaughter of World War I and the intensity of nationalism, a handful of the older generation of reformers such as Kang Youwei advocated for a return to traditional Confucian ideals.

Conclusion

The Chinese were decisively defeated in the Opium War, which led to over one hundred years of weakness. The simplistic interpretation of the Chinese as the hapless victims of greedy foreign invaders is inaccurate. The perception of the Chinese as incapable of using Western weapons and lacking interest in military matters is also inaccurate. First the British and then other European powers and the Japanese had specific advantages in technology during a period in which the Manchu rulers were often philosophically prevented from making meaningful military and political reforms because of their need to appease ethnic Han and Confucian elites. The court eventually adopted Western technologies, suppressed rebellions, and even won land contests against the Russian and the French armies. But they suffered from a period of inefficient rule and unfocused self-strengthening run by territorial politicians who hampered the efforts the rulers did make. After the fall of the last dynasty, China was consumed with civil war that did little to prevent its abuse by outside powers. But it was during this period that one of China's leading political and military figures was revealed.

11

# THE THIRD ENCIRCLEMENT CAMPAIGN

## 1931

This proposal to contend in Jiangxi erred only in setting a time limit of one year. It was based not only on conditions within the province itself, but also on the prospect that a nationwide high tide of revolution would soon arise. For unless we had been convinced that there would soon be a high tide of revolution, we could not possibly have concluded that we could take Jiangxi in a year. The only weakness in the proposal was that it set a time limit of one year, which it should not have done, and so gave a flavor of impetuosity to the word "soon" in the statement, "there will soon be a high tide of revolution." As to the subjective and objective conditions in Jiangxi they well deserve our attention. Besides the subjective conditions described in the letter to the Central Committee, three objective conditions can now be clearly pointed out. First, the economy of Jiangxi is mainly feudal, the merchant capitalist class is relatively weak, and the armed forces of the landlords are weaker than in any other southern province. Secondly, Jiangxi has no provincial troops of its own and has always been garrisoned by troops from other provinces. Sent there for the "suppression of Communists" or "suppression of bandits," these troops are unfamiliar with local conditions, their interests are much less directly involved than if they were local troops, and they usu-

ally lack enthusiasm. And thirdly, unlike Guangdong which is close to Hong Kong and under British control in almost every respect, Jiangxi is comparatively remote from imperialist influence. Once we have grasped these three points, we can understand why rural uprisings are more widespread and the Red Army and guerrilla units more numerous in Jiangxi than in any other province.
    —Mao Zedong, "A Single Spark Can Start a Prairie Fire"

Practice divorced from theory is like groping in the dark; theory divorced from practice is purposeless theory.
    —Zhu De, "Some Basic Principles Concerning Tactics"

S o CLOSE. The Third Encirclement Campaign started only three months after the defeat of the second campaign in July 1931, and it was the first to feature the use of Chiang Kai-shek's loyal divisions and his personal supervision. In this campaign, the Nationalists had cornered a Communist force and seemed poised for victory. As was usually the case, a lone unit, undergunned and with little supply, made a daring escape. It fled quickly to the northeast. Chiang's forces thought this was the fleeing army of Communists and chased them. So far, the third campaign by Nationalist troops, and the fifth if you include campaigns led by warlords and provincial forces, had gone as usual. The Communists outmaneuvered their foe and escaped destruction, and once the core force recuperated, it would spring on the unsuspecting Nationalist troops who had been lured away.

    Before the Long March—in which Communist forces traveled over six thousand miles to escape destruction and restart the revolution in northern China, an action given Valley Forge status among the Chinese—those forces fought a long insurgency. This period saw Mao's first actions as leader of a small insurgency in southern China. After his defeat in the 1927 Nanchang uprising, Mao retreated to the Jinggangshan mountain base. This was a rather impressive mountain range on the western border of Jiangxi. The province itself was somewhat remote but

South China provinces, 1931. Jiangxi was physically remote but still rel-atively close to pivotal cities such as Shanghai, Guangzhou, and Chang-sha. The lack of urban population and industrial workers made it a poor fit for Communist orthodoxy, and the leading Communists grappled with how to best recruit the rural population.

within several hundred miles of pivotal cities such as Shanghai, Changsha, Wuhan, and Guanzhou in southern China. Commu-nist insurgents made sure to possess territory that crossed provincial and county borders, which prevented cooperation among governors. Counterinsurgency soldiers had to advance along limited routes and could be flanked by Communists using secret mountain paths. The Communists then told and retold their exploits against the invaders in rather romanticized fashion to gain even more recruits. Eventually the provinical governors cooperated enough that the Communist forces under Mao and Zhu De (the more-experienced military leader and eventual commander in chief of the Red Army) were forced to make a daring escape along an unused path. After reestablishing a base in the southeastern portion of Jiangxi Province, they were joined by other Communist leaders, and together they expanded their territory and implemented reforms they would later establish on a national scale when they won the civil war in 1949. With Mao rebuilding in a new area, the nominal leader of China, Chiang Kai-shek, finally issued a call for widespread counterinsurgency operations called encirclement or extermination campaigns. Those campaigns did not go well, with the Communists decisively defeating the opposing force using speed and surprise to attack and annihilate Nationalist isolated units. The Communists were finally expelled by the Nationalists in 1934, after the fifth counterinsurgency campaign.

Returning to the third campaign and the Nationalists chasing of a ghost, it seemed to be going the Communists' way again. The Nationalist forces were out of position and exhausted. But Chiang and his lead general, Chen Cheng, managed to salvage what seemed destined to be another defeat. Instead of retreating in disarray as before, Chiang quickly summoned reinforcements, successfully located the Communists' main force, and tightened the noose around it. (See map, page 151.) The Red Army leaders stated in their memoirs that the Nationalist siege was the most difficult and trying time of the extermination campaigns to date.[1] It seemed like Chiang was poised for victory. Unfortunately for him, the Guangxi secession of two southern warlords and the Mukden Incident with Japan that resulted in the creation of the puppet state of Manchukuo ended Chiang's campaign prematurely. Chiang had to contend against external threats and internal revolt from prominent warlords. He was so close to final victory against the Communist insurgency but was denied it at the last moment.

Mao Zedong is hailed in largely hagiographic terms as a result of his eventual ascent to power and victory in the Chinese civil war. His words are immortalized in such texts as *On Guerrilla Warfare* and *On Protracted Warfare*. Revolutionaries like the Vietnamese Ho Chi Minh explicitly credited his theories, and scholars often mention Mao in the same breath as Ernesto "Che" Guevara as leading theorists and practitioners of revolutionary warfare. As Zhu De stated, the theory of warfare without a history of its practice is often groping in the dark.[2] Comparing Communist military campaigns in this period to Mao's widely known theories makes us reexamine both Mao's and Chiang Kai-shek's leadership. His loss in the civil war meant that Chiang is often labeled a failure, while Mao is considered a military genius and great reformer. But these are imperfect perceptions that ignore many details, such as the core Nationalist strength, the favored geographic position of the Communist insurgency, and the unappreciated strategic heritage of the late Qing and Warlord era.

## END OF QING TO THE NANJING DECADE AND INSURGENCY

After the failure of its self-strengthening movement and disastrous defeat by Japan (see chapter 10), the Qing dynasty was in dire straits. It couldn't protect its territory against encroaching Western powers and Japan. The court tried to co-opt the violent antiforeigner uprising called the Boxer Rebellion. Between 1899 and 1901, the violent anti-foreigner movement swept the country, with missionaries killed and the European diplomatic quarters put under siege in Beijing. The Chinese army also placed artillery around and facing the foreign legates. This was the decisive firepower the Boxers needed to overwhelm the besieged Westerners, but the artillery fire was dilatory at best. Besides again giving the Westerners the impression of Chinese martial incompetence, the lackadaisical performance of the artillery is the leading evidence that the court tried to straddle multiple sides by appearing to help the Boxers, who could perhaps solve its problem with the West, while trying to escape blame from Western governments in case the Boxers failed. It also reflected the ongoing strain in the court between belligerent anti-Western factions and those that favored conciliation and reform. A joint operation by Western naval forces and marines quickly landed near Tianjin and fought their way to Beijing. On top of the embarrassment of having such a small army capture its capital, the court did not escape blame for its support of the movement. The Boxer Protocols called for the execution of the officials who supported the rebellion and a payment from the Chinese government larger than its annual tax revenue.

The government limped on for years until it collapsed in 1911. The catalyst was a riot in Sichuan followed by a combination of local gentry, railroad workers, and prominent provincial politicians refusing to obey government edicts. It quickly spread to the general population and led to a mutiny among newly trained military units, whose ethnic Han soldiers had little loyalty to the Manchu dynasty. The last emperor, Puyi, abdicated in 1912. After a short-lived government under Yuan Sikai, the pivotal figure of the period was Sun Yat-sen (1866–1925), considered the father of the Chinese republic, similar to American's reverence for George Washington. The government of Yuan was initially hostile to him, but Sun returned in 1916 and tried to lead the republican government of China. He and his protégé, Chiang Kai-shek, had to lead a fractured country with a rather weak political party and little actual power compared to strong warlords with large and well-equipped armies. The best modernizers in China since the mid-nineteenth century were the provincial governors. When the central government continued to collapse, those modern armies and navies became the basis of their power.

Sun's major beliefs and governing philosophy centered on the three principles: (1) nationalism, or independence from foreign domination, (2) increased prosperity and economic success for each household, largely represented in free trade, and (3) government-sponsored land reform and equal distribution of land, as well as laws to prevent the abuse of what peasants called "evil landlords." In short, Sun tried to alleviate foreign aggression and economic unfairness and inequality that took a financial and emotional toll on large parts of the population. His death due to disease in 1925 left the movement in the hands of Chiang Kai-shek. Because of his time as commandant of the new military academy at Whampoa, he led the Whampoa clique of officers trained at the academy. His northern expedition in 1927 nominally united China (and was only the second time in addition to the Ming dynasty that a southern leader conquered the north to unite China). The year 1927 also marked the beginning of the Nanjing decade. It started with a modest amount of hope for reform and progress under a new government. But Chiang had a difficult time consolidating his rule and implementing reform. He had to fight a Communist insurgency, resist an aggressive Japan, keep the warlords and rival cliques in line, and fight all three threats at the same time as he tried to implement needed reforms.

## THE ENCIRCLEMENT CAMPAIGNS

Chiang considered the Communist threat the greatest to his regime, and in 1930 he tried to suppress that movement throughout China. He assembled troops loyal to him and various warlord-led soldiers to prosecute the campaigns. The limits of Chiang's power are evident in the first campaign. He had to rely on rather ineffective warlord soldiers in his campaigns, and they presented significant challenges. They often fought each other far more than the Communists, and their soldiers lived off the land. Hence, soldiers from other provinces were especially likely to alienate the local population and were considered "guest armies." Bases like the Communists' Jiangxi Soviet, which straddled provincial boundaries, had the advantage of interior lines against divided forces operating in rough terrain. Even if militarily successful, the atrocious behavior of guest armies and their nominal loyalty to Chiang's government made them walking recruiting posters for the Red Army.

There were command and control problems as well. Provincial soldiers received limited equipment and sporadic training that lacked rigor. Even the Nationalist divisions under Chiang often had limited numbers of quality guns, artillery, and radios. The few warlord troops that were highly trained and superbly equipped had leaders more concerned with their own self-interest. Their political power was based in their home provinces and guaranteed by their armed soldiers, so leaders such as Li Zongren of the Guangxi Clique (one of China's more effective generals in the war against Japan) didn't want to risk their political fortunes, and likely their lives, on operations outside of their province. Success against the Communists would only help the national government at the expense of their soldiers, or cost them their armies, political power, and lives upon a defeat.

We might wonder why Chiang used troops of dubious loyalty and effectiveness. He absorbed many of them and transferred them from their bases of operation, which added mass to his operation. If they succeeded, then he would have one less problem and he would get overall credit for the victory. If they failed, the warlords, particularly those from the north, would have less strength with which to oppose him and revolt. Sinologists have listed twenty-seven revolts during the Nanjing decade from 1927–1937, so this wasn't an imaginary concern.[3]

In the First Encirclement Campaign, from December 1930 to January 1931, the warlord troops advancing from the west stopped far away from the battlefield under the pretext of needing supplies, while the troops advancing from the east province never entered Jiangxi to fight the Communists. (See map, page 149.) This left the isolated Eighteenth Army to try to penetrate the areas of Communist control. Even this army group advanced with gaps between its divisions. Hence, it wasn't too difficult for Zhu De and Mao to find, isolate, and annihilate individual divisions. Once they did so, it caused a self-fulfilling prophecy and became vindication for warlords who didn't want to risk their armies. The defections increased when the Communists offered generous terms to defeated Nationalists. And the Red Army scavenged additional weapons, making it even stronger.

The Second Encirclement Campaign occurred from April to May 1931. The important part of this campaign was the east-to-west movement of Communist forces. (See map, page 150.) The forces led by Mao and Zhu preferred to find one isolated unit that had advanced too far and then use the defeat of that unit to cause chaos and undermine the morale of the other units and more easily defeat them. Much like the first campaign, it worked spectacularly. The first defeated unit retreated east and undermined the morale of other units and caused confusion, which led to those units being defeated.

By the Third Encirclement Campaign in July to September 1931, Chiang used more of his own troops loyal to him. While they were more effective than warlord soldiers, this still created its own set of problems. Most historians list this as a Communist victory, but it was at best a draw. Each force received heavy damage and inflicted it on the other, but the Communists were eventually surrounded, and the Nationalists were closing in for the final blow. Chiang had to call off the attack because of outside factors, but he was poised for victory.

Historians normally discuss the campaign, if they discuss it at all, as part of a narrative that results in Communist victory. Because the third campaign is sandwiched between the first, second, and fourth campaigns, and this campaign featured some of the same elements of those Nationalist losses—such as isolated and destroyed divisions, and units that were led astray—it is often considered another Communist victory. But examining the campaign on its own shows that Chiang recovered from setbacks and had a strong position before he had to withdraw on his own accord.

The Fourth Encirclement Campaign was fought from January to March 1933. (See map, page 152.) Note the sixteen-month gap between the third and fourth campaigns. That was because Chiang was dealing with an international crisis and a warlord rebellion. The Communists used this period to expand their support. The fourth is the only campaign in which the Communists didn't lure the Nationalists into rough and distant terrain deep within the province (which theorists called "lure into the deep") to try to isolate and annihilate individual units. Instead, the Communists preemptively attacked Nationalist forces, securing a resounding victory. Because of previous friction with Communist leaders, Mao was not in a position of authority at this time, and because he advocated the exact opposite of the strategy used in this campaign, his leadership was thoroughly discredited. This would be the nadir of Mao's prestige and influence.

The Fifth Encirclement Campaign occurred from September 1933 to October 1934. (See map, page 153.) This campaign lasted almost a year. The Nationalists built blockhouses and slowly advanced into Communist-held territory. They adopted political reforms and an effective economic blockade as the Communists withered trying to attack fixed and fortified positions. This campaign was utterly disastrous for the Communists and forced them to retreat six thousand miles—a trek of twice the width of the continental United States—that became known as the Long March. But Mao benefited once again. Because he was out of favor, he used the defeat to regain power and question the decisions in hindsight to elevate his opinions on what should have been done.

The strategy used most often during these campaigns was called "lure into the deep." The common understanding of this strategy is that under inspiration from Mao, Zhu and other military commanders traded space for time by retreating into the mountainous terrain of the Jiangxi Soviet. The Jinggangshan area especially facilitated this since there were only a few approaches to the mountain villages. In both the Jinggangshan area and the new base established in eastern Jiangxi, the Communists took advantage of poor communication between Nationalist armies. The Nationalist units advanced over rough terrain that strained their logistical capabilities and often isolated individual units. The Communists then used their knowledge of local terrain to mass secretly and annihilate isolated divisions. (Mao might have had this in mind when he later wrote, "Injuring all of a man's ten fingers is not as effective as

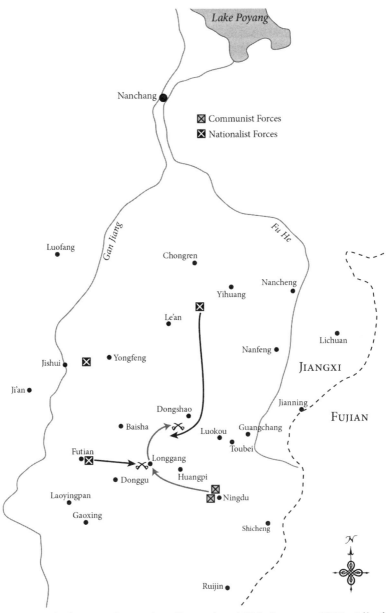

The First Encirclement Campaign, December 1930–January 1931. All of these campaigns occurred in the southeast part of Jiangxi Province. The large gap between the Nationalist forces from the north and west allowed the Communists under Zhu De and Mao Zedong to attack and defeat isolated units at Longgang and Dongshao.

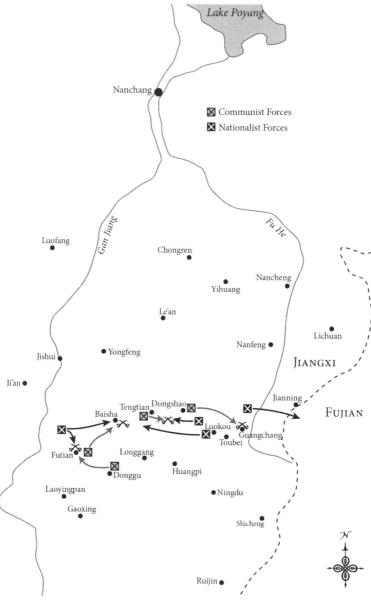

The Second Encirclement Campaign, April–May 1931. The important part of this campaign is the west to east movement of Communist forces. Zhu De believed it was "better to chop off one finger than to wound ten." Communist forces defeated Nationalist units which became isolated after advancing too far at Futian, Baisha, Dongshao, and Guangchang, forcing the Nationalists to flee to Fujian. As each defeated unit retreated east, it undermined the morale of other units and caused confusion which would lead to those units being defeated by the Communists.

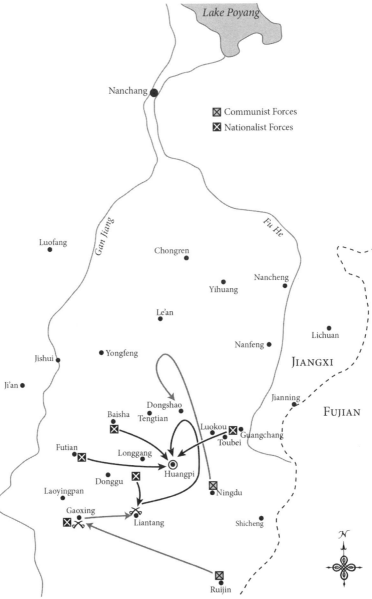

The Third Encirclement Campaign, July–September 1931. This is the first campaign personally led by Chiang Kai-Shek. The Nationalists advanced rapidly and independently to force a decisive battle, which played into Communist strengths. While the Nationalists did have some units isolated, near the end of the campaign, the Nationalists were converging on the main Communist forces at Huangpi. Chiang may have achieved victory at this point but outside events, such as the Mukden Incident, gave the Communists a reprieve, as Chiang was forced to withdraw.

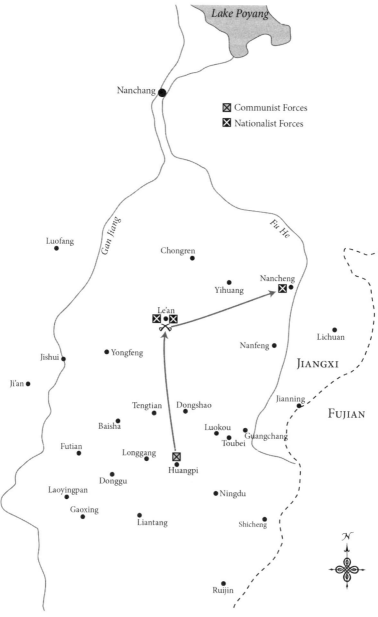

The Fourth Encirclement Campaign, January–March 1933. There was a two year gap between the Third and Fourth campaigns as Chiang was dealing with the Mukden Incident and Guangxi warlord rebellion. The Communists used this period to expand their influence. In this campaign, rather than luring the enemy into the deep, the Communists preemptively attacked Nationalist forces securing a decisive victory at Le'an. Mao was not in a leadership position at this time, and his lure into the deep strategy was discredited.

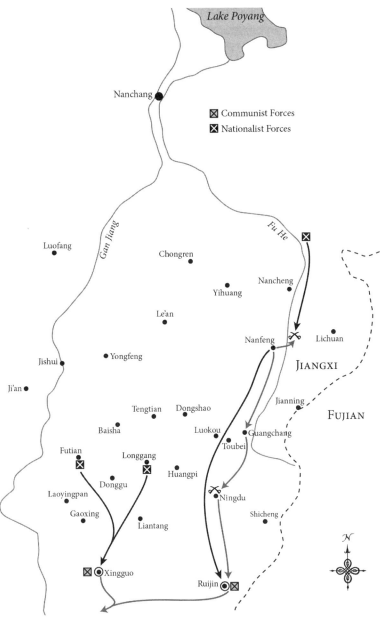

The Fifth Encirclement Campaign, September 1933–October 1934. This final campaign lasted almost a year. The Nationalists built blockhouses and slowly advanced into Communist-held territory, defeating the Communists near Nanfeng and Ningdu. At the same time, they adopted political reforms and created an effective economic blockade against the Communists. This campaign was disastrous for the Communists, forcing them to retreat from Xingguo and Ruijin to begin their Long March. Being on the outside, Mao used this defeat to regain power.

chopping off one.")[4] This created a cascade effect. The defeat of an isolated unit produced a stream of retreating surviving soldiers who would undermine other units with their low morale. In addition, the unit that was destroyed isolated others that depended on it for mutual support. This made the defeat of other Nationalist units easier for the Communists, who then repeated the pattern.

THE NATIONALIST ARMY

The devastating expulsion of the Communists after the Fifth Encirclement Campaign suggests a revision of the common interpretation of the Nationalist armies. The Nationalists were the government that ruled China for over twenty years. They prosecuted successful campaigns to nominally unite the country, control the warlords, expel the Communists, and fight the Japanese. It was only when Chiang Kai-shek initiated the First Encirclement Campaign in late 1930 that the Communist counterinsurgency became a matter of direct concern to the Nationalist government, and it was not until the third campaign in late 1931 that Chiang used higher-quality units. But the limited forces directly loyal to the national government forced the continued use of less-effective warlord troops in each campaign.

The Nationalists had armies capable enough to win against much larger opponents and secure China, but their strengths were uniquely unsuited to combat against the Communists. The Nationalist armies had a diverse composition of units. The core troops most loyal to Chiang often received the best equipment, which created a great deal of jealousy and mistrust, which compounded communication problems, making it difficult to maneuver over large fronts. In the rugged terrain of south China, against an enemy that traded space for time and patiently waited for an isolated unit, a large united front was exactly what was needed, and its absence became a decisive weakness.

Nationalist armies were small and generally had far fewer resources than their opponents. This made them want to end campaigns quickly before they exhausted their supplies. This reinforced the tendency to advance quickly and seek battle, and they often attempted dangerous flank maneuvers to maximize their attacks. Their desire for swift resolution stood in direct contrast to an enemy that had the advantage of withdrawing deep into difficult terrain.

Finally, the Nationalists relied on great élan. Chiang cultivated what he called the Whampoa Spirit in his army. This spirit produced an army with motivated leaders who conducted an aggressive, speedy, and confident pursuit of and engagement with the enemy. Chiang even believed that martial vigor was a model for the nation. Numerous sinologists credit the Whampoa Spirit for the Nationalist's victory against numerically and materially superior opponents. But the Communists often fought with the same amount of élan.[5] The Nationalists couldn't rely on one decisive battle as they had before, but had to contend with a prolonged counterinsurgency against an enemy just as motivated yet better at using the rough terrain to isolate and overwhelm its opponents. Thus, in every way, the factors that made the Nationalist army successful were negated and actually amplified Communist strengths. In contrast to the common view of the Nationalists as perennial losers who were simply placeholders before the inevitable Communist victory, Chiang's military contained many capable and qualified military leaders who often failed because of an impossible combination of intractable problems.[6]

## CULTURAL ENVIRONMENT OF MILITARY WRITINGS

Mao receives a great deal of credit as the father of revolutionary warfare, but there is increasing evidence that questions that image. Scholars are now suggesting that *On Guerrilla Warfare* was written by Zhu De.[7] This volume achieved wide fame during the Greater East Asian War, and many historians and practitioners consider it one of the most succinct, influential, and essential texts on guerrilla warfare. Many of its aphorisms have penetrated popular thought, including the idea that people are like water, and the guerrilla must move through them as freely as a fish through water.

Also quite famous are the sixteen-character formula and the three rules and eight principles. The sixteen-character formula was written in the shape of a classical poem for easy memorization and recitation:

When the enemy advances, we retreat.

When the enemy halts and encamps, we harass them.

When the enemy seeks to avoid battle (becomes tired), we attack.

When the enemy retreats, we pursue.

The three rules and eight points were designed to protect the people against the common depredations of the army. These principles became a concise and profound blueprint for the Red Army in the twenty-year civil war against the Nationalists. And their simple profundity makes them widely applicable around the world. The main rules were essential in helping the Communists win the support of the people. Yet historians also attribute both the sixteen-character formula and main rules to Zhu De.[8] Moreover, even if Zhu gets the credit for these formulations, the main rules had historical antecedents that suggest even Zhu wasn't completely original.

Jiangxi Province had a long history of rebellion. The rugged terrain, limited roads, and bandits who straddled county and provincial jurisdictions made Jiangxi a contested and lawless region that even a strong national government had difficulty controlling. For example, rebels used the Jinggangshan mountain base during the Taiping Rebellion (1850–1864). These rebels even created a set of rules called the Taiping Rules and Regulations that bear an uncanny resemblance to the three main rules and eight principles developed by the Communists.

Guerrilla warfare wasn't new, but Mao often receives credit as the first to fully articulate a theory on protracted revolutionary warfare. However, the eighty years previous to Mao's fight witnessed similar strategic thought in China and Europe. This includes strategies such as lure into the deep, late Qing dynasty military writings, and the theories articulated by Cai E in the early twentieth century and seen later during World War II. Late Qing dynasty (1644–1911) military writings published in 1843 and the mid-1880s discussed these theories. All of them concluded that in the event of war, China should avoid the West's area of strengths, such as naval warfare and ability to bypass coastal defenses. Instead, Chinese forces should draw them into a land battle and use China's vast interior to exhaust them before swarming like "bees and ants." In *On Guerrilla Warfare*, Mao used almost the exact words and stressed the need for the regular army to work with guerrillas to become "gnats biting a giant."[9] While the Qing writers didn't use the phrase "lure into the deep," their methods bear a striking resemblance to those used by Communists in their base areas, and the writings of military thinkers show that the Chinese were not passive victims of the West, but thoughtfully examined the problems and possible solutions to them throughout the nineteenth and twentieth centuries.

The quest for battles of annihilation, or cutting off one finger instead of injuring ten, is not unique either. Qing military theory called for the tactics of "pin down the front and attack the wings and flanks."[10] It is outside the scope of this chapter to show how that applied in conflicts with Japan and France in the late Qing dynasty, but a conflict between southern warlords near Jiangxi province during this turbulent period does include an example of both luring into the deep and a quest for a battle of annihilation. One warlord ordered his troops to retreat a small degree in the face of a frontal attack. His elite troops, prepositioned on the flanks, then enveloped and destroyed the advacing enemy as they were "lured into the deep." Zhu De was considered Mao's right-hand man, and his mentor, Cai E, advanced similar ideas.[11] Like the Qing theorists before him, and Communists and Nationalists after him, he thought that China was too weak to pursue offensive action. They must, Cai argued, use the example of the Boer War and allow the enemy to advance deeply. Then, at the opportune moment, Chinese forces should pounce and destroy them. According to Cai, this would force the enemy into the same fate as Napoleon in Russia and secure victory for China.

It is fairly obvious that using difficult terrain to weaken an enemy before pouncing on it for a complete victory had ample precedent within recent Chinese history. Chiang Kai-shek often withdrew from superior Japanese forces during much of World War II. He moved the capital to the distant city of Chongqing. And Nationalist generals were so good at retreating and then attacking the flanks, such as at the three battles for Changsha, that by the time of Japan's Ichigo offensive, from April to December 1944 (see chapter 12), the Japanese advanced with their strongest forces on the flanks. At the very least, we can safely assume that Mao was not nearly as original and gifted as is commonly assumed and instead engaged in fairly standard practices.

CONCLUSION

The prevailing impressions of Mao Zedong and Chiang Kai-shek suffer from inaccurate perceptions of history. Mao was not nearly the military genius and father of revolutionary warfare that people assume. Chiang was not the corrupt leader of a military junta and ineffectual forces. Mao did end up being the leader of the Communist insurgency and all of China, but it wasn't because of his great military skill. Chiang lost but only after successfully fending off multifaceted challenges that would tax the leader of any state. The next chapter will show the decisive Japanese campaign that fatally weakened Chiang's state.

# THE BATTLE OF HENGYANG OR FOURTH BATTLE OF CHANGSHA

## 1944

First, prior to the Cairo Conference there had been disturbing elements voicing their discontent and uncertainty of America and Great Britain's attitude in waging a global war and at the same time leaving China to shift as best she could against our common enemy. At one stroke the Cairo communique decisively swept away this suspicion in that we three had jointly and publicly pledged to launch a joint all-out offensive in the Pacific.

Second, if it should now be known to the Chinese army and people that a radical change of policy and strategy is being contemplated, the repercussions would be so disheartening that I fear of the consequences of China's inability to hold out much longer.

Third, I am aware and appreciate your being influenced by the probable tremendous advantages to be reaped by China as well as by the United Nations as a whole in speedily defeating Germany first. For the victory of one theater of war necessarily affects all other theaters; on the other hand, the collapse of the China theater would have equally grave consequences on the global war. I have therefore come to this conclusion that in order to save this grave situation, I am inclined to accept your recommendation. You will doubtless realize that in so doing my task in rallying the nation to continue resistance is being made infinitely more difficult.

Because the danger to the China theater lies not only in the inferiority of our military strength, but also, and more especially, in our critical economic condition which may seriously affect the morale of the army and people, and cause at any moment a sudden collapse of the entire front. Judging from the present critical situation, military as well as economic, it would be impossible for us to hold on for six months, and a fortiori to wait till November 1944. In my last conversation with you I stated that China's economic situation was more critical than the military. The only seeming solution is to assure the Chinese people and army of your sincere concern in the China theater of war by assisting China to hold on with a billion gold dollar loan to strengthen her economic front and relieve her dire economic needs. Simultaneously, in order to prove our resolute determination to bring relentless pressure on Japan, the Chinese air force and the American air force stationed in China should be increased, as from next spring, by at least double the number of aircraft already agreed upon, and the total of air transportation should be increased, as from February of next year, to at least 20,000 tons a month to make effective the operation of the additional planes.

In this way it might be possible to bring relief to our economic condition for the coming year, and to maintain the morale of the army and the people who would be greatly encouraged by America's timely assistance. What I have suggested is, I believe, the only way of remedying the drawbacks of the strategy concerning the China and Pacific theaters. I am sure you will appreciate my difficult position and give me the necessary assistance. I have instructed General Stilwell to return immediately to Chungking and I shall discuss with him regarding the details of the proposed changed plan and shall let you know of my decision as to which one of your suggestions is the more feasible.

From the declaration of the Teheran Conference Japan will rightly deduce that practically the entire weight of the United

Nations' forces will be applied to the European front thus abandoning the China theater to the mercy of Japan's mechanized air and land forces. It would be strategic on Japan's part to liquidate the China Affair during the coming year. It may therefore be expected that the Japanese will before long launch an all-out offensive against China so as to remove the threat to their rear, and thus re-capture the militarists' waning popularity and bolster their fighting morale in the Pacific. This is the problem which I have to face. Knowing that you are a realist, and as your loyal colleague, I feel constrained to acquaint you with the above facts. Awaiting an early reply,

—Chiang Kai-shek, reply to US president Franklin Roosevelt

THE CHINESE GENERAL XUE YUE, nicknamed the Patton of Asia, planned a staged withdrawal along the banks of the Xiang River. The forces he commanded couldn't stand against the shock and awe of highly trained and well-equipped Japanese soldiers maneuvering to bring their heavy firepower to bear. But they fought the Japanese as they had been doing since 1937. In the 1944 Ichigo offensive, the wartime government of Chiang Kai-shek faced its greatest threat. In response, Xue planned to overextend the Japanese army, then near Changsha he would attack its flanks, cut its logistical ties where the army was weakest, and force its retreat.

But the Japanese had faced this tactic before. Instead of advancing in three separate columns, with most of the strength in the center, they advanced across a broad front. The strengthened wings were able to repel the Chinese flanking maneuvers. The Japanese advanced against the often-understrength units and captured Changsha. By June 1944, the operation had entered its second phase. But it was largely the same as the first stage. The Chinese forces under Xue held the small city of Hengyang, north of Hunan, with one army and placed thirteen armies on the flanks to try to attack the exposed Japanese flanks. Chiang was under a great deal of pressure to give command of the armies to the American liaison in China, General Joseph Stilwell, and other Chinese generals suggested they strike the Japanese rear. After all, they argued, the Japanese were 212 miles of railroad from their central supply depot and 447 miles of road to their core areas, and they were already short of supplies. But the need to maintain national prestige and defend the city at all costs prevented what might have been the more effective military option.

China's Tenth Army was outnumbered two to one, and its defense of Hengyang, led by Fang Xianjue, lasted forty-seven days and resulted in one of the most ferociously contested battles of World War II. Hengyang was a key rail junction for at least four nearby provinces. And its loss could open up an avenue of approach to the Chinese wartime capital. The Chinese soldiers were told that international prestige was on the line and they held every block. They set up earthworks, trenches, pillboxes, bunkers throughout the urban terrain, and established hidden machine-gun nests around the city.

The Japanese planned to take the city in two days. They started with a massive artillery barrage, absorbed huge counterattacks, and sent mass human wave attacks against the fortified positions in the city. Because of a shortage of ammunition, the Chinese adopted a "three don't" policy: Don't shoot what you can't see, don't shoot what you can't aim at, and don't shoot what you can't kill. This preserved ammunition but also resulted in frequent hand-to-hand fighting. The city was reduced to rubble, and outside the city, thirteen Chinese armies tried to attack the scattered Japanese forces. The Japanese eventually used piles of bodies to scale the Chinese defensive positions. Ultimately the Chinese were forced to retreat after running out of ammunition, but their fierce fighting displayed Chinese bravery and desire to resist the foreign invaders. The concentrated forces of the Japanese, and failure to coordinate the relief efforts of surrounding Chinese units with the relieving armies, meant that Chinese forces were defeated piecemeal. The political pressure Chiang was under and the strained relationship with Xue Yue illustrated the difficulties Chiang had ruling China during the Nanjing decade and throughout World War II and the civil war. His disagreements with Stilwell represented the conventional but mistaken view of Chinese weakness and supposed lack of desire to fight. The Battle of Hengyang, or Fourth Battle of Changsha, was one of the most desperately fought and intense conflicts of the entire war, yet few outside of China seem to know about it or care.[1]

## THE COURSE OF THE WAR

Some scholars date the beginning of this Sino-Japanese conflict to the Mukden Incident of 1931, with Japan's annexation of Manchuria, but active fighting between Japan and China was imminent when a Japanese training exercise engaged Chinese soldiers in July 1937 at the Marco Polo Bridge southwest of Beijing. This incident finally sparked war in northern China. The Nationalist army on the eve of the war had tried to strengthen itself but still had numerous flaws. The soldiers received poor training and the officers' training was uneven. The German-taught officers at the Baoding and Whampoa academies were generally better trained, but there simply weren't enough qualified officers to staff and lead 130 divisions. Their tactics were out of date, they were poorly supplied, and they lacked a general staff. Staff positions were not seen as desirable assignments for qualified officers, so the posts usually became patronage positions for the relatives of officers. This meant that even well-trained and well-equipped units weren't employed in well-organized operations. The headquarters units often failed to distribute vital but relatively scarce equipment such as anti-aircraft and antitank guns and key artillery pieces.[2] Chinese divisions were smaller than their Japanese counterparts, but because of differences in training, equipment, and doctrine, it generally took three and as many as ten Chinese divisions to counter one Japanese division.[3]

Chiang Kai-shek wanted to relieve pressure on the northern front near the Marco Polo Bridge and gain international support for his position by attacking Japanese positions in Shanghai. Unfortunately, the battle became a meat grinder for the best-trained units. A combination of the dense urban terrain, stiff Japanese defense, and a failure to distribute artillery and air assets from headquarters to forward units meant the Chinese were not initially effective. Eventually, the Japanese flanked Chinese positions with two amphibious landings. The Chinese retreated in disarray to Nanjing.

During the headlong retreat, motivated Chinese generals tried to stem the tide by regrouping behind the "Chinese Hindenburg Line," a series of fortifications designed to provide a defense in depth. Yet the Japanese advance was so swift that Chinese officials with the keys to these fortifications had also fled. The resulting chaos meant that Chinese units couldn't establish strong positions and Japanese troops quickly flanked them, forcing them to retreat again. The series of forts designed to produce a stalemate with the Japanese was breached in less than two weeks. A combination of Japanese skill and Chinese ineptitude led to the premature end of this siege, the fall of the southern capital at Nanjing (Nanking), and a series of abuses to the civilian population called the rape of Nanjing.

At this point, Chiang became even more reliant on a coalition of warlord troops. The execution of General Han Fuju seemed to have a catalyzing effect that helped his leadership. Han had abandoned a key position in northern China without firing a single shot. After his death, other generals started to coalesce and fight the key Battle of Wuhan. The superior performance of these now-motivated warlord generals led some scholars to criticize the Whampoa clique that Chiang preferred. In addition to the effective warlord generals, the Baoding clique, named after the German-led military academy founded in 1921, were far less political and more professional than the Whampoa clique. Despite the differences in background and mistrust of each other, in 1938, around Wuhan, they started to establish an effective resistance.[4] (The Communists were active in this period as well. But they were rebuilding their strength after the grueling Long March and avoided major pitched battles, but they did score a famous victory against a Japanese supply train strung out along Pingxingguan Pass in late 1937.) The Japanese planned to have their units in northern and southern China perform a pincer operation and capture the city of Wuhan. After the fall of much of northern China and key cities in southern China, this was the center of Chinese political, industrial, and military strength. It was here that the Chinese achieved one of their first major victories of the war, at Taierzhuang.

The city of Taierzhuang was on the eastern bank of the Grand Canal, not that far from where Manchu Bannermen were humiliated one hundred years before. Among the forces in charge of the defense was Li Zongren, leader of the Guangxi clique whose rebellion forced Chiang to abort the Third Encirclement Campaign. The city was located near a pivotal railroad junction flanking Xuzhou. The capture of Taierzhuang opened a path along the railroad to Xuzhou and then Wuhan. After a ten-month campaign in 1938, Xuzhou and eventually Wuhan were lost, but the vigorous defense showed Chinese strength and earned grudging respect from world observers. The lack of an early knockout for Japanese forces led to several years of strategic indecision.

The Japanese army trained for rapid, explosive offensives whereby it maneuvered its impressive firepower into position to blast its enemies. The Japanese army was not trained for garri-

Overleaf: China during World War II. After the encirclement campaigns, the Communists moved to northern China on the Long March. Until 1941, they joined a united front with the Nationalists against the Japanese. The Japanese invaded in 1937 near Beijing and Shanghai. Japanese forces quickly overran the Chinese along the coastal regions and the flat north. After the rape of Nanjing and fall of Wuhan in 1938, the Chinese government fled to Chongqing. Outside of limited offensives by the Japanese and guerrilla warfare by the Chinese, the front settled down by 1939. The Japanese wanted to bring China to its knees through bombing, with Chongqing being a major target, but failed to do so. The 1944 Ichigo offensive had several divergent goals including creating a continuous strip of occupied land from north China to Vietnam, and the capture of Allied airbases attacking Japan. The Japanese did achieve some of the offensive's objectives, but were checked at several points, including at Hengyang; soon Allied bombers were operating from Pacific Islands, reducing the strategic importance of the airfields in China.

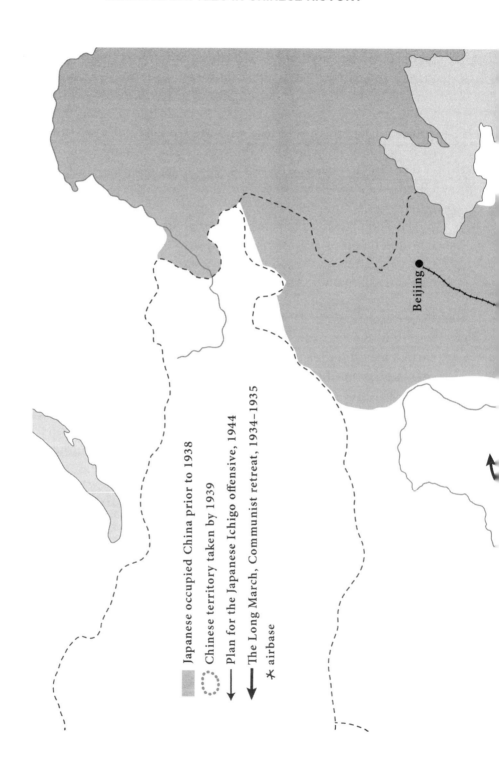

Japanese occupied China prior to 1938

Chinese territory taken by 1939

Plan for the Japanese Ichigo offensive, 1944

The Long March, Communist retreat, 1934–1935

✱ airbase

Beijing

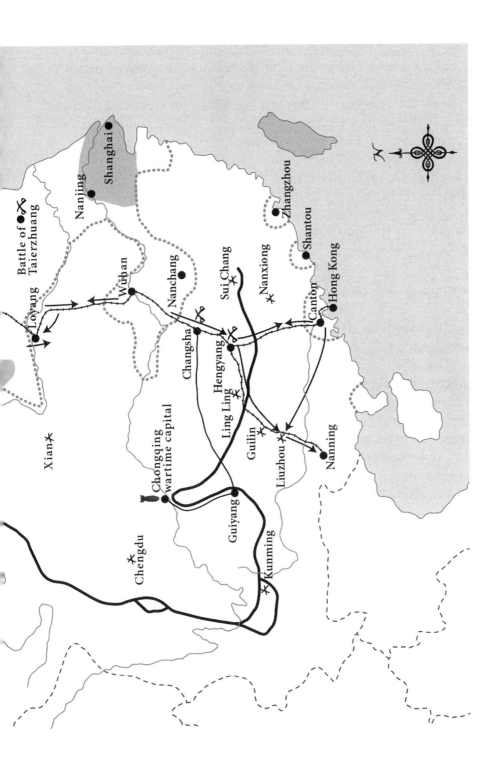

son duty or counterinsurgency. They had first-class weapon systems superior to what the Chinese had and disciplined junior officers and noncommissioned officers. But their spectacular initial victories concealed structural weaknesses. Outside of winning in those quick-strike offensives, such as their speedy victory against China in their 1894–1895 war, they did not have a long-term strategy to deal with China. They ended up alternating between additional quick strikes and heavy bombing of Chinese areas. Eventually the Chinese found that it was best to place a modest holding force in front of the Japanese advance, offer substantive but still token resistance, and let a much larger flanking force attack them when the Japanese thrust seemed to reach its logistical limit. This happened in several battles for Changsha. Its remote location and difficult terrain made it a reach for Japanese forces, and the Chinese often chose this spot to engage the Japanese. By the time of the Ichigo offensive, they had already fought the Fourth Battle of Changsha.

The Ichigo offensive was designed by the Japanese to decisively solve Japanese strategic problems. The Japanese naval fleet and merchant marine were suffering severe losses at the hands of American naval forces, so they wanted to clear and hold a contiguous land route connecting all of Japanese territory from northern China to Indo-China. They also wanted to destroy American bomber bases in China that were pummeling the Japanese homeland.

This campaign featured over five hundred thousand Japanese soldiers, comparable in size to the German invasion of the Soviet Union. It devastated China and destroyed key industrial areas in Nationalist territory. This operation laid to waste an estimated 25 percent of China's industrial base. Tax revenue dropped sharply, critical shortages of food resulted from loss of grain areas, and over one million Chinese soldiers were killed just in that year. Chiang wrote, "I'm 58 years old this year, of all the humiliations I have suffered in my life, this is the greatest. . . . 1944 is the worst year for China in its protracted war against Japan."[5]

Most critically for postwar China, Chiang had to withdraw the small portion of his forces keeping a wary eye on the Communists. (About 30 out of 130 divisions kept them under control.) The Communists took advantage of the absence of Nationalist and Japanese forces in the region to expand greatly. They took over Japanese-based territories and supplies that had been vacated or abandoned. The Communists were the true winners of the Ichigo offensive.

### RISE OF COMMUNIST FORCES

Once World War II had started, Chiang and Mao Zedong formed an uneasy united front that lasted until 1941. The nature of what triggered the collapse of their cooperation is disputed, but either Nationalist treachery or Communist insubordination rising to the level of mutiny inspired an armed response from Nationalist units. When it was finished, over seven thousand members of the Communists' New Fourth Army were killed, and the unified government fell apart. The Communist guerrilla forces had much more success and were much better at advertising their successes during the war against Japan. The Nationalist army units caught behind enemy lines or entrapped by swift Japanese thrusts also formed guerrilla units. But they were committed to holding key territory and performing large unit operations. Nationalist guerrillas were inept at doing the political work needed to gain support of locals, and even though official publications stressed concern for local populations, the Nationalist commanders often ignored them. In 1938, the Nationalists had over seven hundred thousand men behind Japanese lines, but by 1943, they had no meaningful forces remaining to wage guerrilla warfare.[6]

In contrast, by 1945, after the Ichigo offensive, Communist guerrilla forces had grown to nine hundred thousand that formed the core of mobile Communist strength and about three million local forces that often supplied intelligence and guarded key terrain for the mobile units. The three rules and eight principles and other easily digested concepts helped them expand influence and win the support of the population. By the end of

World War II, the Communists had secured much of the Japanese industry in Manchuria. There was an uneasy period of peace as negotiations were led by American general George C. Marshall. But fighting renewed in 1948. The Nationalist industries had a difficult time recovering from the damage of the Ichigo offensives, and well-planned strikes led by Communist-infiltrated unions led to key labor strife. Combined with defections of Nationalist units, the Nationalist government lost the civil war and fled to Taiwan.

WESTERN ASSUMPTIONS ABOUT THE WAR

Contrary to popular belief—shaped by the memoirs of a bitter General Stilwell—Chiang was committed to fighting the Japanese, not just hoarding material for the eventual fight with the Communists. As shown by the furious resistance in Hengyang, the active guerrilla war, and the carnage from the Ichigo offensive, the Nationalists fought for their nation with over a million soldiers giving their lives. Chiang bravely resisted Japanese aggression as early as 1937, long before the Western powers joined the war against Japan or Germany. China suffered greatly, fought longer, and fought just as bravely as the Western allies. It even fought the Communists long before the Cold War had started. Chiang led a fractured government that was beset with jealousy, mistrust, and competing agendas among warlords, Communists, and Nationalists against one of the best armies in the world, and he had to fight with extremely limited resources. Hue Yue, for example, was a trusted associate of Chiang's who served in the northern expedition, but he and other generals wanted Chiang to fight the Japanese more than the Communists, and Hue actually threatened to arrest Chiang during the Xian Incident (1937) if he didn't form a united front with the Communists. This made for rather tense relations, as the political leader had to direct and coordinate strategy throughout the war with a general who tried to arrest him.

Strategically, China was put on the back burner during the war. American strategy in the Pacific such as island hopping, the bombing of the Japanese homeland, and destruction of shipping is credited with winning the war. But the war in China occupied the majority of Japanese army units and exhausted some that were scheduled to assist Japanese offensives in the Pacific, including the Battle of Guadalcanal (August 1942–February 1943). Chinese officials argued after the war that if resources for Pacific island-hopping offensives in 1944 had been given to them, they could have stopped the Ichigo offensive and could have protected American bomber bases in China. There is merit to this argument, as China actually received a relatively small amount of Lend-Lease material until 1945, by which point the outcome of the war was no longer in doubt.[7]

The arguments about military aid were vigorously disputed by Western analysts at the time, with most viewing China, and Chiang in particular, as backward, feudal, and corrupt. This was simply an inaccurate judgment. Chiang led vigorous training programs supervised by German officers before and during the early parts of the war. (This led to the somewhat ironic situation in which German advisers were placed in Chinese units fighting their future Japanese allies.) He had rather strong ideas for reform, but because of a violent insurgency and then an aggressive world war on his doorstep, he was unable to implement vital changes like land reform. There is also a bit of Western stereotyping of what "modern" is. China, while still largely agricultural, already had a strong body of ancient and modern strategic thought, and the Nationalists showed élan and competence in the northern expedition and securing the country during the Nanjing decade (see chapter 11.)

Stilwell's disagreements with Chiang, and many journalists who lapped praise on what they viewed as Communist reformers, helped solidify the Western view of China as an incompetent military regime,[8] but the Chinese prosecuted the war using various strategies to mobilize support, maintain armies, and fight battles. Nationalist propaganda looked at various national heroes, ranging from Sunzi to Yue Fei to Qi Jiguang to help rally resistance. Their economy sometimes moved to a barter system so the government could get needed funds. Up until the Ichigo offensive, the Nationalist government stabilized farm production and tax revenues and essentially turned the war into a stalemate (though part of that was a result of the lack of Japanese strategy to end the war). Figures vary widely, but an estimated ten million soldiers and twenty million civilians were killed in what is sadly and unfairly seen by many historians as a fruitless Chinese contribution to World War II.[9]

## CHINA STRATEGY AFTER THE WAR AND BRIEF APPLICATION FOR THE UNITED STATES

Once China did become united under one ruler, it became surprisingly aggressive. Many analysts thought China would spend many years recovering its strength. But in the very first years of the new regime, the Chinese almost immediately began to reassert their traditional territorial rights. Many apologists for Chinese policy like to point to China's one hundred years of weakness and Western imperialism to justify its behavior, but the specific situations in each of these postwar conflicts point to Chinese aggression. In the last sixty years, the Chinese have fought offensive wars against every one of their neighbors, on their opponents' territory.

Immediately after winning the Chinese civil war, Mao launched a sneak attack in Korea. US general Douglas MacArthur was approaching the Yalu River with the ostensible goal of unifying the Korean Peninsula under a democratic government, but the Yalu was also the border with China, and this was an indirect confrontation with the Communist regime. Mao and the Communists had just won a civil war that was embedded in a regional and world war with Japan. Their economy was a wreck, which meant that fighting a war so quickly was not in China's interest. Moreover, even if they did choose to fight, it was a preemptive attack outside their territory. A surprise attack against approaching American forces seems less justified considering the reasons China had for avoiding war, and its preemptive nature.

A few years later, Mao seized islands claimed by Taiwan. The Communists had massed forces in the area and were ready to seize the main island and destroy the remnants of Chiang's Nationalist forces. They clearly broadcast their objectives by radio to the Chinese people. Further operations were curtailed by the timely intervention of American forces in the Taiwan Strait and even the threat of nuclear warfare from the administration of President Dwight Eisenhower. This protected Chiang's regime and led to the situation today where the People's Republic of China claims Taiwan as part of its nation and will eventually be unified with it.

China also sought to readjust what it called unequal treaties (the first of which ended the Opium War). One of these was made with the British regarding India. During a contentious dispute, China preemptively attacked India in 1962. Chinese forces, operating in high altitude, stormed across the border and seized the territory of Aksia Chin that it claimed was unfairly taken by the British during their imperialist expansion in the nineteenth century. After a month, the two countries declared a ceasefire.

Upon victory in the 1962 Sino-Indian War, Chinese leaders became increasingly bellicose in their demands to adjust their borders to counter former treaties. As early as 1950, Mao sought to adjust China's borders. He and Stalin, however, affirmed the existing line between China and the Soviet Union in the Sino-Soviet Treaty of Friendship of 1950. But Mao still believed they were open to adjustment based on terms of mutual respect for territorial integrity found within the treaty. Over the next decade, both sides increased their forces along the central Asian border. This included the disputed islands in the Ussuri and Amur Rivers, the border with Mongolia, and the Xinjiang-Kazakhstan region (including the Ili region, where Russia and China had fought in the nineteenth century). Soviet troop strength went from seventeen divisions in 1965 to twenty-seven in 1969 to forty-two divisions numbering almost one million men by the mid-1970s. The Soviets also stationed several divisions in Outer Mongolia and a significant nuclear arsenal. These forces clashed with local Chinese citizens in minor border incidents throughout the mid-1960s, especially in Xinjiang Province but also the border between islands running through the Ussuri and Amur Rivers.

In addition to thousands of minor incidents, the armies clashed twice during March 1969 along the rivers. On March 2, soldiers of the Chinese People's Liberation Army (PLA) attacked Damansky (Zhenbao) Island. Supported by artillery and heavy guns on their side of the shore, they failed to resist Soviet attempts to retake the island. As many as sixty Russians died in this encounter. (Conflicting sources and government secrecy make an exact count difficult.) Early on the morning of March 15, the PLA attacked again. It committed a regiment consisting of two thousand soldiers against Soviet defenses. The Chinese did not capture the island and sustained eight hundred casualties to the Soviets' sixty. The Chinese, though, gained by showing their willingness and ability to face the Soviets in combat. This directly challenged the 1968 Brezhnev Doctrine, which in practice meant that any deviance from Communist orthodoxy was considered a threat to the Soviet Union and subjected the threat to armed intervention. While the PLA did not win, the existence of battles between it and a superpower enhanced its reputation. The Chinese also signaled their intention to counter Soviet influence in Central and East Asia. The tension continued throughout the 1970s as both sides added more soldiers and nuclear weapons. The Chinese added an extensive series of bunkers and moved their nuclear weapons facility to Tibet. The Chinese also became responsive to American overtures. President Richard Nixon and Secretary of State Henry Kissinger worked to exploit the rift in Sino-Soviet relations and weaken the Soviet Union. China sought closer relations with America and Japan to isolate Soviet allies in Southeast Asia.

The tensions continued between the two Communist powers in late 1979, when Chinese forces attacked Vietnam. The war was little more than a border clash, and the Chinese claim they didn't seek any territory, but they were left in possession of the disputed territory that Vietnam held at the beginning of the war. Combined with their previous behavior against every one of their neighbors, a particular pattern emerged.

The Chinese claimed they were acting defensively. Given their recent and distant past, they had some reason for their concern. But their strategic maneuvers fighting preemptive offensive actions against their neighbors suggest they will continue to make aggressive moves while claiming them to be defensive actions. Currently, their attention is on the South China Sea, where they are building up islands also claimed by the Philippines and Japan, with weapons that can be used to interdict shipping or launch attacks from a forward position. They have also begun construction on their first aircraft carrier. Policy makers can't be cowed into a passive stance by Chinese claims of victimhood, when the last sixty years of Communist leadership in China has shown a fondness for provocative offensive action.

CONCLUSION

China fought Japan hard during World War II but their contribution to the Allied victory was unfairly considered negligible. The Battle of Hengyang, or Fourth Battle of Changsha, was decisive in helping to crystallize attitudes that the Chinese should be proactive in defending their country and avoid repeating the one hundred years of weakness that they had endured. But following the war, that policy has tended to lead to aggressive, preemptive incidents.

China has a long history of military conflict. They have their own venerable military legacy, some of which is widely read around the world for use in non-martial professions. The simple profundities of those writings contain valuable messages, but are also subject to change with the time. The Chinese also have a legacy of connections between geography and military technology, ranging from groups of crossbowmen that are ideal for breaking up large infantry groups, to the use of large heavy canon in sieges, and bows against nomadic horsemen.

They have a martial, cultural, political, and philosophical legacy that is largely underappreciated, particularly given a new and seemingly aggressive China. After reading this book the reader should have a better grasp of the myths and realities in Chinese history. They have suffered at Western hands, but they also had specific ethnic tensions that prevented reform, and during their long history they often subdued or displaced nearby rivals. They have specific cultural legacies like the bandwagon effect of dynastic change, but they are not immune to the disintegrating and unifying effects of military power.

# NOTES

INTRODUCTION

Epigraph: "The Break-Up of China, and Our Interest in It," *Atlantic Monthly* 84, no. 502 (August 1899): 276–280.

1. A good book that shows how Chinese officials were far more practical and realistic in their war making than the stereotypical portraits painted of biased Confucian historians can be found in Peter Lorge ed., *Debating War in Chinese History* (London: Brill, 2013).

2. Richard Overy, *A History of War in 100 Battles* (New York: Oxford University Press, 2014).

3. Richard Holmes and Martin Evans, eds., *A Guide to Battles: Decisive Conflicts in History* (Oxford: Oxford University Press, 2009).

CHAPTER 1: THE BATTLE OF MALING, 342 BC

Epigraph: Ralph Sawyer, trans., *The Six Secret Teachings of Tai Kong*, in *The Seven Military Classics of Ancient China* (Boulder, CO: Westview Press, 1993), 73.

1. For a historical account mixed with Chinese literary ideas, see Sima Quan, *Records of the Grand Historian*, 3 vols., trans. Burton Watson (New York: Columbia University Press, 1961).

2. Ralph Sawyer, trans., *The Seven Military Classics of Ancient China* (Boulder, CO: Westview Press, 1993).

CHAPTER 2: THE BATTLE OF RED CLIFFS, 208

Epigraph: Han Feizi, excerpt from Albert Craig, *The Heritage of Chinese Civilization* (New York: Prentice Hall, 2000, 22. Cao Cao, "Short Song Style," anon. trans., accessed July 17, 2017, https://en.wikisource.org/wiki/Translation:Short_Song_Style.

1. For a discussion of the defensive advantages of ships tied together, see Rafe de Crespigny, *Generals of the South*, Internet edition (Canberra: Australian National University, 2004), 169–173.

2. Rafe de Crespigny, an Australian sinologist, has done a lot of excellent work on this period. His copious research and translations of primary sources are available online at the Australian National University, https://openresearchrepository.anu.edu.au/html/1885/42048/index.html, accessed July 14, 2017.

3. Stuart Schram, *The Thought of Mao Tse-tung* (London: Cambridge University Press, 1989), 54. Mao made many contradictory statements, but his theoretical training and writing was rather sparse in the early years. See chapter 11.

## CHAPTER 3: THE BATTLE FOR LUOYANG IN THE WAR OF THE EIGHT PRINCES, 302–305

Epigraph: Reprinted in David Graff, *Medieval Chinese Warfare: 300–900 AD* (New York: Routledge, 2002), 47.

1. For one of the only English summaries, see Edward Dryer, "Military Aspects of the War of the Eight Princes: 301–307," in *Military Culture in Imperial China,* ed. Nicola Di Cosmo (Cambridge, MA: Harvard University Press, 2009), 112–142.

2. John Lynn, *Battle: A History of Combat and Culture* (Boulder, CO: Westview Press, 2003), 1–28, directly addressed Hanson's argument, though the central thesis of the book indirectly argues against any particular way of war.

## CHAPTER 4: THE BATTLE OF FEI RIVER, 383

Epigraph: Herbert Giles, trans., "The Peach-Blossom Fountain," by Tao Qian, in *Gems of Chinese Literature* (Shanghai: Kelly and Walsh, 1922), 102–104. Ralph Sawyer, trans., "Sun-Tzu's Art of War," in *The Seven Military Classics of Ancient China* (Boulder, CO: Westview Press, 1993), 172.

1. Michael Rogers, "The Myth of the Battle of the Fei River," *T'oung Pao,* 2nd ser., vol. 54 (1968): 50–72.

2. David Graff, *Medieval Chinese Warfare: 300–900* (New York: Routledge, 2002), 64–70.

## CHAPTER 5: THE BATTLE OF YAN ISLAND, 589

Epigraph: Herbert Giles, trans., "Drunk-Land," by Wang Qi, in *Gems of Chinese Literature* (Shanghai: Kelly and Walsh, 1922), 109–111. Ralph Sawyer, trans., "Sun-Tzu's Art of War," in *The Seven Military Classics of Ancient China* (New York: Westview Press, 1993), 164.

1. Arthur Wright, "The Sui Dynasty," *The Cambridge History of China*, vol. 3, *S'ui and Tang China, Part 1*, ed. Dennis Twitchett (Cambridge: Cambridge University Press, 1979), 48–149.

2. Stephen Averill, *Revolution in the Highlands: China's Jinggangshan Base Area* (Lanham, MD: Rowman and Littlefield, 2006). See part 1 in Averill's book for an extensive discussion of the role of the *hakka* and the socioeconomic background of the Communist insurgency.

3. Empress Dowager Imperial Edict, November 21, 1899, in Stanley Smith, *China from Within: The Story of the China Crisis* (London: Marshall Brothers, 1901), 149.

4. Michael Lowe, "The Campaigns of Han Wudi," in *Chinese Ways in Warfare*, ed. Frank A. Kierman and John K. Fairbank (Cambridge, MA: Harvard University Press, 1974), 67–122.

CHAPTER 6: THE BATTLE OF HULAO, 621

Epigraph: Frits Holm, *The Nestorian Monument: An Ancient Record of Christianity in China, with Special Reference to the Expedition of Frits V. Holm*, ed. Paul Carus and Alexander Wylie (Chicago: Open Court Publishing, 1909),18–19.

1. For a full discussion of the campaign leading to the Battle of Hulao, see David Graff, "Dou Jiande's Dilemma: Logistics, Strategy, and State Formation in Seventh-Century China," in *Warfare in Chinese History*, ed. Hans Van De Ven (London: Brill, 2000), 77–105.

2. Graff, *Medieval Chinese Warfare*, 174.

3. For more discussion and copious notes about Sunzi's teachings, textual variants, and commentaries from Chinese scholars, see Ralph Sawyer, trans., *The Seven Military Classics of Ancient China* (Boulder, CO: Westview Press, 1993).

4. Barbara Tuchman, *A Distant Mirror: The Calamitous 14th Century* (New York: Knopf, 1978), 246–268. "[Lord Coucy] could neither take up arms against his father-in-law, to whom he owed fealty for his English lands, nor, on the other hand, fight against his natural liege lord, the King of France." An accessible example of balancing competing duties to rival sovereigns includes the work on the French De Coucy family that held allegiances to both the French and English kings by birth and marriage respectively.

5. Albert Dien, "The Stirrup and Its Effect on Chinese Military History," in *Warfare in China to 1600*, ed. Peter Lorge (New York: Ashgate, 2005), ch. 9.

6. This story of the training of a samurai and a detailed discussion of samurai arc in Karl Friday, *Samurai, Warfare, and the State in Medieval Japan* (New York: Routledge, 2003).

## CHAPTER 7: THE SIEGE OF XIANGYANG, 1267–1273

Epigraph: *The Book of Ser Marco Polo: The Venetian Concerning Kingdoms and Marvels of the East*, vols. 1 and 2, trans. and ed. Colonel Sir Henry Yule (New York: Charles Scribner's Sons, 1903), accessed July 17, 2017, http://afe.easia.columbia.edu/mongols/pop/menu/class_marco.htm. Yue Fei, *The Whole River Red*, Morgan Deane trans., "Man Jiang Hong," accessed July 4, 2017, https://en.wikipedia.org/wiki/Man_Jiang_Hong.

1. Huang K'uang-Chung, "Mountain Fortress Defense: The Experience of the Southern Song and Korea in Resistingthe Mongol Invasions," in *Warfare in Chinese History*, ed. Hans Van De Ven (Cambridge, MA: Harvard University Press, 2001), 222–251.

2. Peter Lorge, *The Asian Military Revolution: From Gunpowder to the Bomb* (New York: Cambridge University Press, 2008), 7–44.

3. Peter Lorge, *War, Politics, and Society in Early Modern China: 900–1795* (New York: Routledge, 2005), 58–77.

## CHAPTER 8: THE BATTLE OF LAKE POYANG, 1363

Epigraph: Peter Lorge, *War, Politics and Society in Early Modern China: 900–1795* (New York: Routledge, 2005), 98. John Mansfield, *Marco Polo's Travels* (New York: Dent and Sons, 1918), 300.

1. Edward Dreyer, "The Poyang Campaign of 1363: Inland Naval Warfare in the Founding of the Ming Dynasty," in *Chinese Ways in Warfare*, ed. Frank A. Kierman and John K. Fairbank (Cambridge, MA: Harvard University Press, 1974).

2. Peter Lorge, "Water Force and Naval Operations," in *A Military History of China*, ed. David Graff and Robin Higham (New York: Westview Press, 2002), 81–96.

3. Kenneth Chase, *Firearms: A Global History to 1700* (Cambridge: Cambridge University Press, 2003), 28–52.

4. Ibid., 25, lists the steps from a 1607 training manual.

## CHAPTER 9: THE SIEGE OF PYONGYANG, 1593

Epigraph: Kenneth Swope, "Crouching Tigers, Secret Weapons: Military Technology Employed During the Sino-Japanese Korean War, 1592–1598," *Journal of Military History* 69, no. 1 (2005): 11–41. Kenneth

Chase, *Firearms: A Global History to 1500* (Cambridge: Cambridge University Press, 2008), 150.

1. Kenneth Swope, *A Dragon's Head and a Serpent's Tail: Ming China and the First Great East Asian War, 1592–1598* (Norman: University of Oklahoma Press, 2012), 284–300.

2. Kenneth Swope, "Cutting Dwarf Pirates Down to Size: Amphibious Warfare in Sixteenth-Century East Asia," in *New Interpretations in Naval History: Selected Papers from the Fifteenth Naval History Symposium Held at the United States Naval Academy 20–22 September 2007*, ed. Yu Maochun (Annapolis, MD: Naval Institute Press, 2009), 81–107.

3. Kenneth Swope, "A Few Good Men: The Li Family and China's Northern Frontier in the Late Ming," *Journal of Ming Studies* (2004): 34–81.

4. Morgan Deane, "Forming the Formless," in *Ender's Game and Philosophy* (New York: Blackwell, 2013), 78–88.

5. Ralph Sawyer, "Sun-Tzu's Art of War," in Sawyer, *Seven Military Classics*, 159.

6. Ibid., 158.

7. Tai Kong, *The Six Secret Teachings of Tai Kong*, in Sawyer, *Seven Military Classics*, 66.

8. Alastair Iain Johnson, *Cultural Realism: Strategic Culture and Grand Strategy in Chinese History* (Princeton: Princeton University Press, 1998), 155.

9. Ibid., 62.

10. Sawyer, *Seven Military Classics*, 164, 165, 168.

11. Sawyer, "Sun-Tzu's Art of War," 183.

12. Kenneth Swope, "Manifesting Awe: Grand Strategy and Imperial Leadership in the Ming Dynasty," *Journal of Military History* 79, no. 3 (July 2015): 597–634, 605.

CHAPTER 10: THE BATTLE OF ZHENJIANG, 1842

Epigraph: *Sources of Chinese Tradition: From 1600 through the Twentieth Century*, comp. Wm. Theodore de Bary and Richard Lufrano, 2nd ed., vol. 2 (New York: Columbia University Press, 2000), 269–270. Albert Craig, *The Heritage of Chinese Civilization* (New York: Prentice Hall, 2000, 122.

1. Bruce Elleman, *Modern Chinese Warfare, 1795–1989* (New York: Routledge, 2001), 13–56.

2. Ibid., 71–115.

3. Richard Horowitz, "Beyond the Marble Boat: The Transformation of the Chinese Military, 1850–1911," in *A Military History of China*, ed.

David Graff and Robin Higham (Boulder, CO: Westview Press, 2002), 153–174.

CHAPTER 11: THE THIRD ENCIRCLEMENT CAMPAIGN, 1931

Epigraph: Mao Zedong, "A Single Spark Can Start a Prairie Fire," in *Selected Military Writings of Mao Tse-tung* (Beijing: Foreign Language Press, 1967), 75. Mao Zedong, *On Guerrilla Warfare*, trans. Samuel Griffith (New York: Praeger, 2007). Zhu De, "Some Basic Principles Concerning Tactics" (1933), in *Selected Works of Zhu De* (Beijing: Foreign Language Press, 1986), 24.

1. Wilbur Hsu, *Survival through Adaptation: The Chinese Red Army and the Encirclement Campaigns, 1927–1936* (printed by author, 2012), 88.

2. Zhu De, "Some Basic Principles Concerning Tactics" (1933), in *Selected Works of Zhu De* (Beijing: Foreign Language Press, 1986), 24.

3. William Wei, *Counterrevolution in China: The Nationalists in Jiangxi during the Soviet Period* (Ann Arbor: University of Michigan Press, 1985), 41.

4. Mao Zedong, "Problems of Strategy in China's Revolutionary War," in *Selected Military Writings of Mao Tse-tung* (Beijing: Foreign Language Press, 1967), 146.

5. Peter Worthing, "Continuity and Change: Chinese Nationalist Army Tactics, 1925–1938," *Journal of Military History* 78 (2014): 998.

6. Colin Green, "Turning Bad Soldiers into Polished Steel: Whampoa and the Rehabilitation of the Chinese Soldier," in *Beyond Suffering: Recounting War in Modern China*, ed. James Flath and Norman Smith (Vancouver: University of British Columbia Press, 2011), 153–185. The title of this article is rather clever, as it takes a Chinese proverb denigrating the military—"Good iron doesn't make good nails, and good men don't make good soldiers" (see chapter 4)—and turns the denigrated soldiers into polished, or good, steel.

7. Stuart Schram, *The Thought of Mao Tse-tung* (Cambridge: Cambridge University Press), 52.

8. Matthew William Russell, "From Imperial Soldier to Communist General: The Early Career of Zhu De and His Influence on the Chinese Army" (PhD diss., George Washington University, 2009), 75.

9. Mao, *On Guerrilla Warfare*, 92.

10. Russell, "Imperial Soldier," 230.

11. Agnes Smedley, *The Great Road: The Life and Times of Chu Teh* (New York: Monthly Review Press, 1956), 226. On that page, Smedley

relates that they were considered two arms of one person and were often called Zhu Mao by the people.

## CHAPTER 12: THE BATTLE OF HENGYANG OR FOURTH BATTLE OF CHANGSHA, 1944

Epigraph: "Generalissimo Chiang Kai-shek Reply to US President Roosevelt," Dec. 9, 1943, https://en.wikisource.org/wiki/Generalissimo_Chiang_Kai-shek_reply_to_US_President_Roosevelt.

1. Wang Qisheng, "The Battle of Hunan and the Chinese Military's Response to Operation Ichigo," in *The Battle for China: Essays on the Military History of the Sino-Japanese War of 1937–1945*, ed. Edward Drea, Hans Van DeVen, and Mark Peattie (Stanford, CA: Stanford University Press, 2011), 403–420.

2. Peter Harmsen, *Shanghai 1937: Stalingrad on the Yangtze* (New York: Casemate, 2015), 52.

3. Chang Jui-Te, "The Nationalist Army on the Eve of the War," in *The Battle for China: Essays on the Military History of the Sino-Japanese War of 1937–1945*, ed. Edward Drea, Hans Van De Ven, and Mark Peattie (Stanford, CA: Stanford University Press, 2011), 83–104. Sections 1 and 2 provide several excellent chapters that detail the political background and respective organization, equipment, and shortcomings of the Japanese and Chinese armies at the start of the war.

4. Stephen MacKinnon, *Wuhan 1938: War, Refugees, and the Making of Modern China* (Los Angeles: University of California Press, 2008), 31–43.

5. Qisheng, "Battle of Hunan," 403.

6. Yang Kuisong, "Nationalist and Communist Guerrilla Warfare in North China," in *The Battle for China: Essays on the Military History of the Sino-Japanese War of 1937–1945*, ed. Edward Drea, Hans Van De Ven, and Mark Peattie (Stanford, CA: Stanford University Press, 2011), 308–327.

7. Lend-Lease was the program developed by President Franklin Roosevelt's administration to provide much-needed war supplies such as oil, food, trucks, and military hardware to Britain, the Soviet Union, China, and eventually dozens of countries during World War II.

8. Edgar Snow, *Red Star over China: The Classic Account of the Birth of Communism,* rev. ed. (New York: Grove, 1994), and Smedley, *Great Road*, 86. Both texts present very sympathetic views of Communists. An example is Smedley's reference to Zhu De reading seminal texts by George

Washington and Montesquieu's *Spirit of the Laws* by the soft glow of the moonlight.

9. *The Battle for China: Essays on the Military History of the Sino-Japanese War of 1937–1945*, ed. Edward Drea, Hans Van De Ven, and Mark Peattie (Stanford, CA: Stanford University Press, 201), 421–484, is an excellent assessment of China's contribution in World War II, China's wartime experience contextualized in world history, and the war's meaning in Chinese history.

# BIBLIOGRAPHY

Averill, Stephen. *Revolution in the Highlands: China's Jinggangshan Base Area*. Lanham, MD: Rowman and Littlefield, 2006.

Chase, Kenneth. *Firearms: A Global History to 1700*. Cambridge: Cambridge University Press, 2003.

Craig, Albert. *The Heritage of Chinese Civilization*. New York: Prentice Hall, 2000.

Crespigny, Rafe de. *Generals of the South*. Internet edition. Canberra: Australian National University, 2004.

De, Zhu. *Selected Works of Zhu De*. Beijing: Foreign Language Press, 1986.

Deane, Morgan. "Forming the Formless." In *Ender's Game and Philosophy*. Edited by Kevin Decker, 78–88. Malden, MA: Blackwell, 2013.

Dien, Albert. "The Stirrup and Its Effect on Chinese Military History." In *Warfare in China to 1600*. Edited by Peter Lorge. New York: Ashgate, 2005.

Drea, Edward , Hans Van De Ven, and Mark Peattie, eds. *The Battle for China: Essays on the Military History of the Sino-Japanese War of 1937–1945*. Stanford, CA: Stanford University Press, 2011.

Dreyer, Edward. "Military Aspects of the War of the Eight Princes, 301–307." In *Military Culture in Imperial China*. Edited by Nicola di Cosmo, 112–142. Cambridge, MA: Harvard University Press, 2009.

———. "The Poyang Campaign of 1363: Inland Naval Warfare in the Founding of the Ming Dynasty." In *Chinese Ways in Warfare*. Edited by Frank A. Kierman and John K. Fairbank. Cambridge, MA: Harvard University Press, 1974.

Elleman, Bruce. *Modern Chinese Warfare, 1795–1989*. New York: Routledge, 2001.

Empress Dowager Imperial Edict, November 21, 1899, in Stanley Smith, *China from Within: The Story of the China Crisis* (London: Marshall Brothers, 1901), 149.

Friday, Karl. *Samurai, Warfare, and the State in Medieval Japan.* New York: Routledge, 2003.

Graff, David. "Dou Jiande's Dilemma: Logistics, Strategy, and State Formation in Seventh-Century China." In *Warfare in Chinese History.* Edited by Hans Van De Ven, 77–105. London: Brill, 2000.

———. *Medieval Chinese Warfare: 300–900.* New York: Routledge, 2002.

Graff, David, and Robin Higham, eds. *A Military History of China.* Boulder, CO: Westview Press, 2002.

Green, Colin. "Turning Bad Soldiers into Polished Steel: Whampoa and the Rehabilitation of the Chinese Soldier." In *Beyond Suffering: Recounting War in Modern China.* Edited by James Flath and Norman Smith, 153–185. Vancouver: University of British Columbia Press, 2011.

Hanson, Victor Davis. *Carnage and Culture: Nine Landmark Battles in the Rise of Western Power.* New York: Anchor Books, 2002.

Harmsen, Peter. *Shanghai 1937: Stalingrad on the Yangtze.* New York: Casemate, 2015.

Holmes, Richard, and Evans, Martin, eds., *A Guide to Battles: Decisive Conflicts in History.* Oxford: Oxford University Press, 2009.

Horowitz, Richard. "Beyond the Marble Boat: The Transformation of the Chinese Military, 1850–1911." In *A Military History of China.* Edited by David Graff and Robin Higham. Boulder, CO: Westview Press, 2002.

Hsu, Wilbur. *Survival through Adaptation: The Chinese Red Army and the Encirclement Campaigns, 1927–1936.* Printed by author, 2012.

Johnson, Alastair Ian. *Cultural Realism: Strategic Culture and Grand Strategy in Chinese History.* New York: Princeton University Press, 1998.

Jui-Te, Chang. "The Nationalist Army on the Eve of the War." In *The Battle for China: Essays on the Military History of the Sino-Japanese War of 1937–1945.* Edited by Edward Drea, Hans Van De Ven, and Mark Peattie, 83–104. Stanford, CA: Stanford University Press, 2011.

Kierman, Frank A., and John K. Fairbank, eds. *Chinese Ways in Warfare*. Cambridge, MA: Harvard University Press, 1974.

K'uang-Chung, Huang. "Mountain Fortress Defense: The Experience of the Southern Song and Korea in Resisting the Mongol Invasions. In *Warfare in Chinese History*. Edited by Hans Van De Ven, 222–251. London: Brill, 2000.

Kuisong, Yang. "Nationalist and Communist Guerrilla Warfare in North China." In *The Battle for China: Essays on the Military History of the Sino-Japanese War of 1937–1945*. Edited by Edward Drea, Hans Van De Ven, and Mark Peattie, 308–327. Stanford, CA: Stanford University Press, 2011.

Lorge, Peter. *The Asian Military Revolution: From Gunpowder to the Bomb*. New York: Cambridge University Press, 2008.

———. *War, Politics and Society in Early Modern China: 900–1795*. New York: Routledge, 2005.

———. *Warfare in China to 1600*. New York: Ashgate, 2005.

———. "Water Force and Naval Operations." In *A Military History of China*. Edited by David Graff and Robin Higham, 81–96. Boulder, CO: Westview Press, 2002.

———, ed. *Debating War in Chinese History*. London: Brill, 2013.

Lowe, Michael. "The Campaigns of Han Wudi." In *Chinese Ways in Warfare*. Edited by Frank A. Kierman and John K. Fairbank, 67–122. Cambridge, MA: Harvard University Press, 1974.

Lynn, John. *Battle: A History of Combat and Culture*. Boulder, CO: Westview Press, 2003.

———. "The Embattled Future of Academic Military History." *Journal of Military History* 61, no. 4 (Oct. 1997): 777–789.

MacKinnon, Stephen. *Wuhan 1938: War, Refugees, and the Making of Modern China*. Los Angeles: University of California Press, 2008.

Mao Zedong. *On Guerrilla Warfare*. Translated by Samuel Griffith. New York: Praeger, 2007.

Overy, Richard *A History of War in 100 Battles* New York: Oxford University Press, 2014.

Qisheng, Wang. "The Battle of Hunan and the Chinese Military's Response to Operation Ichigo." In *The Battle for China: Essays on the Military History of the Sino-Japanese War of 1937–1945*. Edited by Edward Drea, Hans Van De Ven, and Mark Peattie, 403–420. Stanford, CA: Stanford University Press, 2011.

Quan, Sima. *Records of the Grand Historian*. 3 vols. Translated by
Burton Watson. New York: Columbia University Press, 1961.

Rogers, Michael. "The Myth of the Battle of the Fei River." *T'oung
Pao*, 2nd ser., vol. 54 (1968): 50–72.

Russell, Matthew William. "From Imperial Soldier to Communist
General: The Early Career of Zhu De and His Influence on the Chinese Army." PhD diss., George Washington University, 2009.

Sawyer, Ralph D., trans. *The Seven Military Classics of Ancient China*.
Boulder, CO: Westview Press, 1993.

Schram, Stuart. *The Thought of Mao Tse-tung*. Cambridge: Cambridge University Press, 1989.

Smedley, Agnes. *The Great Road: The Life and Times of Chu Teh*.
New York: Monthly Review Press, 1956.

Snow, Edgar. *Red Star over China: The Classic Account of the Birth
of Communism*. Rev. ed. New York: Grove, 1994.

Swope, Kenneth. "Crouching Tigers, Secret Weapons: Military Technology Employed during the Sino-Japanese-Korean War, 1592–
1598." *Journal of Military History* 69, no. 1 (2005): 11–41.

———. "Cutting Dwarf Pirates Down to Size: Amphibious Warfare
in Sixteenth-Century East Asia." In *New Interpretations in Naval
History: Selected Papers from the Fifteenth Naval History Symposium Held at the United States Naval Academy 20–22 September
2007*. Edited by Yu Maochun. Annapolis, MD: Naval Institute
Press, 2009.

———. *A Dragon's Head and a Serpent's Tail: Ming China and the
First Great East Asian War, 1592–1598*. Norman: University of
Oklahoma Press, 2012.

———. "A Few Good Men: The Li Family and China's Northern
Frontier in the Late Ming." *Journal of Ming Studies* (2004): 34–81.

———. "Manifesting Awe: Grand Strategy and Imperial Leadership
in the Ming Dynasty." *Journal of Military History* 79, no. 3 (July
2015): 597–634.

Tuchman, Barbara. *A Distant Mirror: The Calamitous 14th Century*.
New York: Knopf, 1978.

Van De Ven, Hans. "The Sino-Japanese War in History." In *The Battle
for China: Essays on the Military History of the Sino-Japanese War
of 1937–1945*. Edited by Edward Drea, Hans Van De Ven, and
Mark Peattie, 446–466. Stanford, CA: Stanford University Press,
2011.

Van De Ven, Hans, ed. *Warfare in Chinese History*. London: Brill, 2000.

Wei, William. *Counterrevolution in China: The Nationalists in Jiangxi during the Soviet Period*. Ann Arbor: University of Michigan Press, 1985.

Worthing, Peter. "Continuity and Change: Chinese Nationalist Army Tactics, 1925–1938." *Journal of Military History* 78 (2014): 995–1016.

Wright, Arthur. "The Sui Dynasty." In *The Cambridge History of China*. Vol. 3, *S'ui and Tang China, Part 1*. Edited by Dennis Twitchett. Cambridge: Cambridge University Press, 1979.

———. "Problems of Strategy in China's Revolutionary War." In *Selected Military Writings of Mao Tse-tung*, 77–146. Beijing: Foreign Language Press, 1967.

———. "A Single Spark Can Start a Prairie Fire." In *Selected Military Writings of Mao Tse-tung*, 65–76. Beijing: Foreign Language Press, 1967.

Zhu De, "Some Basic Principles Concerning Tactics" (1933). In *Selected Works of Zhu De*. Beijing: Foreign Language Press, 1986, 24.

# INDEX